LITERACY CHANGEMAKERS

Also Available

Breaking Through the Language Arts Block:
Organizing and Managing the Exemplary Literacy Day
Lesley Mandel Morrow, Kenneth Kunz,
and Maureen Hall

Literacy Changemakers

Bringing the Joy of Reading
and Writing into Focus
for Teachers and Students

Kenneth Kunz
Maureen Hall
Rachel Lella

Foreword by Diane Lapp

THE GUILFORD PRESS
New York   London

Copyright © 2021 The Guilford Press
A Division of Guilford Publications, Inc.
370 Seventh Avenue, Suite 1200, New York, NY 10001
www.guilford.com

Printed in the United States of America

This book is printed on acid-free paper.

Last digit is print number: 9   8   7   6   5   4   3   2   1

Library of Congress Cataloging-in-Publication Data

Library of Congress Cataloging-in-Publication Data
Names: Kunz, Kenneth, author. | Hall, Maureen P., author. | Lella, Rachel, author.
Title: Literacy changemakers : bringing the joy of reading and writing into focus
    for teachers and students / Kenneth Kunz, Maureen Hall, Rachel Lella ;
    foreword by Diane Lapp.
Description: New York : The Guilford Press, 2021. | Includes bibliographic
    references and index.
Identifiers: LCCN 2020031606 | ISBN 9781462544509 (paperback) |
    ISBN 9781462544547 (hardcover)
Subjects: LCSH: Language arts (Elementary) | Reading (Elementary) | Language
    arts (Secondary) | Reading (Secondary) | English language—Study and
    teaching—Foreign speakers.
Classification: LCC LB1576 .K865 2021 | DDC 372.6—dc23
LC record available at *https://lccn.loc.gov/2020031606*

About the Authors

Kenneth Kunz, EdD, is Assistant Professor of Literacy/Language Arts at Monmouth University and serves as co-president of the New Jersey Literacy Association. He is also on the board of the International Literacy Association and the advisory board of the Rutgers Center for Literacy Development. Dr. Kunz began his career as a third-grade teacher in the New Jersey Public Schools and was recognized as an outstanding teacher through the New Jersey Governor's Teacher Recognition Program. He was also awarded an Edward Fry Fellowship in Literacy at Rutgers, The State University of New Jersey. Dr. Kunz is a coauthor of *Breaking Through the Language Arts Block: Organizing and Managing the Exemplary Literacy Day* and the founder of For the Love of Literacy, LLC (*www.fortheloveofliteracy.net*). He has served in the roles of teacher, reading specialist/coach, school administrator, district administrator, and teacher educator.

Maureen Hall, EdS, is a literacy coach in several districts across New Jersey through her work with the Rutgers Center for Literacy Development and with For the Love of Literacy, LLC. She is co-president of the New Jersey Literacy Association and serves on the advisory board for the Rutgers Center for Literacy Development. Ms. Hall is a coauthor of *Breaking Through the Language Arts Block: Organizing and Managing the Exemplary Literacy Day*. She was recognized as an outstanding teacher through the New Jersey Governor's Teacher Recognition Program and has served in the roles of teacher, reading specialist/coach, school administrator, district administrator, and teacher educator.

Rachel Lella, EdD, is Supervisor of Elementary Education and K–12 English as a Second Language in the Wall Township (New Jersey) Public Schools and serves on the board of the New Jersey Literacy Association. She found a passion for education after seeking a career change, and began working with preschool students before teaching third- and fourth-grade language arts/literacy in a Title I district, where she had the opportunity to work closely with multilingual learners and their families. Dr. Lella is a recipient of a scholarship from the Rutgers Center for Literacy Development and an Edward Fry Fellowship in Literacy at Rutgers, The State University of New Jersey. She has served in the roles of teacher and district administrator.

Foreword

The authors of *Literacy Changemakers: Bringing the Joy of Reading and Writing into Focus for Teachers and Students* invite us to answer the question *Why do I teach?* As I paused to do so, I thought about myself as a young midwestern girl, who every Saturday would gather all my neighborhood pals together to play my favorite game—School—with me playing the role of teacher, of course. Each week, anticipating that I could convince my fellow players to participate, I searched for a good book, often a comic book, that I could read to them to keep them motivated long enough to fulfill my need to teach. Even though I knew nothing about purposeful lesson planning, as I struggled to keep my friends motivated I learned the value of prereading the text. This way I could be prepared to ask questions that got them to talk, and also I could practice reading before sharing. I always had crayons and paper for them to draw a response to share. Even with all my efforts, I was usually able to keep them interested for only 30 minutes or so before my brother would suggest we all go to a nearby field to play baseball, ride our bikes, or play other games.

Even though I loved playing School, I'm not sure if, at that young age, I could have fully answered the question *Why do I teach?* In the years since, I know that I teach for two big reasons. I teach so that I can share new ideas with my students, whether they are 4 years old or 40, in ways that promote their love of learning and cause them to continue growing as thinkers and problem solvers. I also teach because, even though this profession is both challenging and rewarding, it has always given me joy. My sister once told me that few people can say that about their jobs or careers. I believe most teachers can!

When I finished reading *Literacy Changemakers*, I knew I had to broaden the focus of the authors' invitational question *Why?* by sharing with you that the most important *why* of this text is *why you must read it,* and *why* doing so will propel your base of knowledge about literacy instruction and about yourself as an educator. As this book clearly demonstrates, you have a daily opportunity to be a changemaker for your students and colleagues and yourself.

Think about the term *changemaker*. I think it captures exactly why most of us decided to become teachers. We believe that through our instruction we are able to ensure learning for all our students and that this learning will profoundly change their worlds. Fortunately, this book validates this belief and offers us many, many ideas that enable us to do our jobs more effectively so that each student has an equitable path to learning and each community of educators joins forces to ensure this.

The first realization you will have as you read *Literacy Changemakers* is *why* you must become a member of a school community. The reason is that, as a team sharing a sense of camaraderie with your colleagues, you will be even more effective at promoting literacy for every child. As the authors of this book illustrate, together you and your colleagues can gain shared insights and knowledge needed to make literacy the reality for every student. You will create a school vision and a community that promotes learning equity and inclusion. No child or colleague will be left out.

When I read the Preface, I was a little skeptical that the authors could successfully convey, in one book, the two bodies of information they intended to share. The first is to share instructional ideas for teaching literacy; the other is to promote the power of, and need for, school collegiality. These sounded like two different goals to me. Usually a book is either about literacy instruction or about another topic, such as collegial work. Well, this book thoroughly teaches us about *both* areas and does it so well that you will feel you have the knowledge needed to be a changemaker among your colleagues and also, through instruction, for your students.

I finished this book with enriched ideas about literacy instruction, inclusiveness, English learners, and team building through listening, supporting, and collaborating. I also finished believing the book should be read and discussed in professional learning communities. I believe it could move any teacher, team, or school administrator closer to identifying and planning how to attain collaborative goals, with the result that every student continues to achieve.

If you aren't sure where to begin planning such goals, you will certainly develop them as you glide through the powerful instruction in each chapter. I must confess I thought I would skim the chapters to get ideas about what to write in this Foreword. But the authors' tone drew me in. I wanted to be a participating colleague. I felt like I would be a bad team member if I didn't read and consider all the instructional ideas presented in each chapter! Thank heavens I read it closely, because I have certainly added to and refined many of my instructional ideas, especially ideas about how to be a member of a collaborative team. As I read this book, I was able to evaluate my knowledge about teaching literacy and also about being a contributing community member. I layered new ideas, insights, and questions on what I already know. This book was professional development for me, and I was excited about the new learning I gained.

Professional development is so important to us as a community because most of us begin our careers with only three to six units of literacy instruction. This is why I chuckle when I hear that teachers who have had only three units of literacy instruction are being criticized for not knowing how to assess, plan, and manage instruction that accommodates all the students' differences in their classrooms. Imagine if you visited any other professional who had taken only one or two introductory courses in their specialty. You would be outraged. When I think about all I have learned since my first reading methods course, I am extremely thankful that my initial professor said many, many times: "This course is the beginning of all the knowledge you will need to ensure that you know how to plan instruction to support all the students you will meet in your career." I continue this path of learning by reading books like *Literacy Changemakers.* The authors have done an excellent job of offering both initial knowledge for new teachers and deeper knowledge for ongoing learning about ways to support literacy growth across the grades for English speakers and multilingual students—and how to do this as part of a collegial team.

It is not obvious that three authors wrote this book. It has one unified voice, which exemplifies the unification that these authors suggest should exist among school and classroom teams. They don't just tell us to be collaborative. They show us how and explain why doing so matters to the growth of our colleagues and our students.

You can begin answering your own *Why?* by completing the introductory chart shown in Chapter 4. First assess yourself as a member of your school team and then, through the rest of the book, learn how to add to both your cognitive and social–emotional growth, with an end goal of becoming a participating member of your school team, dedicated to expanding literacy learning for all your students.

Assess yourself to determine if you need knowledge expansion or even an "attitude readjustment." And be sure that your colleagues are not spending so much time addressing your issues that they move their focus away from the children. As you read the examples of collegiality shared in this book, self-evaluate to assess if you need to redesign your participation to be a more supportive member of your school team. Doing so will help you identify your professional and instructional questions, set professional goals, and self-monitor to confirm if these goals are being accomplished.

The authors of this book teach us how to self-reflect on our goals, motives, and paths, and also how to support our students in identifying their goals, making a plan, and monitoring accomplishments. They provide us with ideas about how to retool when the progress isn't linear. They teach us how to invite goal-setting collaboration among students, with the end result being the students' vested interest in learning goals because they have helped identify them. With your guidance as educators, the students have ownership of their learning process.

To share some additional pieces of knowledge you will learn from reading this book, I use another activity that I call *I Think You'll Learn...*

I think you'll learn that these authors don't just inform us about what is needed to be a powerful team member. Instead they provide examples and data collection tools and show us how to differentiate the process for each member of the team. I think you'll learn . . .

- why teams matter.
- how to create school teams.
- how to get reluctant school participants to embrace the joy of becoming a school literacy team member.

- a plethora of useful tools to assess for both instructional planning and students' literacy achievement.
- how to welcome English learners by engagement in a "Bienvenidos Book Club."
- how to use formative assessment ideas, such as anecdotal notes taken during your reading groups, strategy groups, one-on-one conferring, and students' comments while conferring.

But remember, becoming a participating member of a school team is only one major focus area of this book. I think you'll learn that another is reevaluating and expanding your knowledge of how to support students as they learn to read, learn to *love* to read, and become part of a community of literate scholars. Whatever your grade level, the authors have included ideas that will help you assess and then teach every student in your classroom. You won't finish this book viewing your assessment, planning, and instructional practices as isolated components. You will instead have an integrated understanding of language, writing, and reading and how to work with your colleagues to ensure that every child in your school has equitable opportunities to grow. This is because the authors suggest setting goals for students that support them in accomplishing their grade-level standards. They provide instructional examples that are the antithesis of a lockstep, staircase approach to success. Instead they show us how to identify the strengths and needs of each student and then provide instruction that scaffolds each toward success.

This book doesn't just offer these insights regarding students; it shows us how to engage ourselves and our communities in a team approach with a plan that identifies what we each need to do to grow as literacy leaders and teachers. *The focus is always on the student*—but in order to support students and teachers, we must evaluate ourselves, what we know, and our attitudes about learning new information and about being a team player. The authors call this an *asset mindset*. They say that "with an asset mindset, we see where the student is. We see where we are, and we design a plan for forward movement toward identified goals." With a deficit mindset, we see where the student is not, and we never consider our role in the game of learning. Just imagine how powerfully impacted the atmosphere of our classrooms and schools would be if we valued both our colleagues *and* the students' assets, priorities, and needs, alongside our own expectations for excellence. The authors of this book have given us a path, a plan, and encouragement to be better members of our instructional teams and better teachers. The tone of this book is one of joy because it is chock full of real-world ideas that will indeed work for you, your faculty, and your students. When you finish reading this book, you will reaffirm your pride in being a team player and, above all, an educator who has never taken your eyes off the learning paths of your students.

I hope you will enjoy, as much as I did, reading this book and experiencing your own professional development while doing so.

DIANE LAPP, EdD
Distinguished Professor of Education, San Diego State University
Instructional Coach and Teacher, Health Sciences High and Middle College

Preface

Literacy Changemakers: Bringing the Joy of Reading and Writing into Focus for Teachers and Students is written for teachers who embrace the research supporting the need for an exemplary literacy day and a comprehensive literacy program. This book takes a panoramic look at *changemaking* through the lens of a collaborative literacy team working together to positively impact readers and writers across diverse school communities. Whether you are a teacher-leader, school administrator, district administrator, literacy coach, literacy specialist, or professional developer, *Literacy Changemakers* will guide you to think about refocusing joy when it comes to teaching literacy. This book is appropriate for teachers at all levels of experience, reading/literacy specialists and coaches, administrators, future teachers, and anyone advocating for literacy for all.

WHAT MAKES THIS BOOK DIFFERENT?

This book stresses the importance of literacy interwoven with quality leadership and a passion for making a difference in the lives of readers and writers. It is aimed at anyone hoping to ignite a spark of inspiration in local school communities. What's unique is that it speaks to literacy changemakers in a way that feels like a cheerleading voice is in your head, repeatedly chanting: *Find joy! Go literacy! You've got this!*

Features of the book include:

- **Inspirational quotes** to spark curiosity and a thought-provoking jump into the topics presented in each chapter.
- **Vignettes** at the beginning of each chapter that follow a collaborative decision-making process in a team-structure approach (featuring real literacy leaders), inviting the reader to observe collective efforts focused on making positive changes on behalf of readers and writers in classrooms and schools.

- **A light-bulb symbol** denoting some of our favorite "Lit Ideas," or practical tips that literacy changemakers can use immediately with students to make this work happen.
- A **Stop, Think, and Take Action** section at the end of each chapter, which includes a set of tips and reflective questions that guide the next steps literacy changemakers should take in bringing a joy for reading and writing back into classrooms, schools, and local communities. Consider it a call to action for classroom teachers, teacher-leaders, literacy specialists, literacy coaches, school administrators/leaders, district administrators/leaders, and literacy professional developers.

Chapter 1 discusses the importance of shared literacy leadership and getting literacy advocates involved in this worthwhile work. It introduces the importance of identifying with your "why" and building a collaborative and connected team whose core mission and values are clear. A review of the exemplary literacy day for grades K–12 teaches us to begin with the end in mind.

Chapter 2 reveals that engagement and joy must be at the core of all of our planning and thinking about literacy instruction in schools and classrooms. Ingredients for finding that joy and sample activities for promoting positive collaboration around literacy initiatives are discussed. A variety of initiatives and activities, including the International Literacy Association's Children's Rights to Read, are explored.

Chapter 3 encourages literacy changemakers to gain a better understanding of the school or district's literacy "story" and to use data as a way to drive change rather than simply to document or measure success. It provides ways for changemakers to get a feel for the literacy landscape and guiding questions for how to conduct an English language arts (ELA) program evaluation, if needed. Ideas for looking into a more accurate and comprehensive literacy picture beyond test scores are included, along with suggestions for ensuring that all students are taken into account when considering the strengths and needs of the school community.

Chapter 4 ignites a positive energy for professional development (PD) and teacher-centered professional learning. Whether you are a literacy professional developer, a member of a PD team, or some other form of literacy changemaker, the advice in this chapter will serve you well. After an initial description of the naysayers and negative beliefs about PD, we immediately move into practical and research-based support for creating an enjoyable atmosphere for learning.

Chapter 5 invites the reader into joyful learning environments that are purposefully structured to enhance engagement and students' literacy learning. The elements of culture, climate, access to books, print, space, and time that characterize these environments are discussed. A new checklist tool for designing classroom libraries to be more interdisciplinary and inclusive is shared.

Chapter 6 sets the stage for recalibrating literacy instruction for early learners. Ideas for promoting joy and happiness are introduced, and ways to use the reading foundational standards to engage students are discussed. Sample activities for developing phonological awareness, phonemic awareness, and phonics are summarized. In addition, readers are introduced to sample vocabulary meetings and ideas for engaging read-alouds that take students' reading interests into account. Suggestions related to writing for authentic purposes are included throughout the chapter.

Chapter 7 is a call to action, addressing the fact that reading is on the decline among adolescents. Ideas related to bringing vocabulary words and independent reading to life are presented with an eye toward sustained engagement. The latest information for book clubs is shared, and unique perspectives from an exemplary teacher are included as she "pulls out all the stops" for ensuring that the needs of readers in the upper grades are met with joy and excitement.

Chapter 8 advocates for meeting the needs of multilingual learners and begins with an asset-based mindset for welcoming learners with diverse language needs in the classroom. Engaging activities for fostering a sense of belonging in the learning environment are provided. The reader is encouraged to get to know the learner beyond the label and to empower families through active involvement. A variety of resources are shared.

Chapter 9 explains the importance of family literacy and of tapping the potential of parents. It begins with an explanation of students' rights to integrated support systems and how we can utilize a variety of structures to increase parent, family, and community engagement. A number of successful project ideas and suggestions for increasing involvement are shared.

Chapter 10 introduces various forms of new literacies and technology. We discuss the use of new literacies for the future and describe a plethora of engaging activities, such as getting digital with mentor texts, utilizing diverse media formats, and finding apps and digital tools that work for our readers and writers. An authentic list of popular tools and resources gathered from our literacy community are shared.

In Concluding Thoughts, we summarize the key points of the previous chapters and present information about how literacy changemakers can get involved in joyful practices, while promoting students' comprehensive literacy development.

Acknowledgments

We would like to extend our heartfelt appreciation to our community of literacy friends who bring us joy in our daily positive interactions. These are not the folks who "yes" us to death or nitpick the nitty-gritty, but the folks who lift us up when we are in need of a refocus on joy and doing what's best for readers and writers within our school communities. They not only contribute to our evolving understanding of an exemplary literacy day, but also join us in this worthwhile work with energy so positive that it's contagious.

We would like to start by thanking the real-life literacy leaders you will read about in our vignettes at the beginning of each chapter. These folks, known as the "Hatchery Hill Six," are Mrs. Griffin, Mrs. Diskin, Mrs. Calabrese, Mrs. Rosenfeld, Mrs. Schiano, and Mrs. DeMarco. They are a big part of the reason that New Jersey leads when it comes to literacy achievement in the United States, and their commitment to helping all students achieve their potential is unwavering.

A special "thank-you" is in order for Jaclyn Wilson, a research graduate assistant from Monmouth University, who fielded calls or texts from our writing team on weekends, always answering with an upbeat attitude. Her work led to new insights in the book, including ideas for bringing joy to the lives of multilingual readers and writers.

We extend the same Monmouth University gratitude to Dr. Jason Fitzgerald and Dr. Michelle Schpakow. They add a love for linguistics and interdisciplinary approaches to this amazing work, and, because of their collaboration, we think about literacy, language, and the literacy environment in new ways, especially as they relate to the classroom library.

Additional thanks are in order for Brian Benavides, Lindsay Bernero, Dr. Remi Christofferson, Gena Cooley, Erin Embon, Matt Kukoda, Jane Losinger, Nicole

Mancini, Kathy McCue, and Elaine Mendez. Their practical tips from literacy leadership and teacher leadership perspectives are amazing, once again demonstrating how to lead from the heart. We can only hope we did their work justice in showing how their examples shine across the chapters.

We also thank the board members of the International Literacy Association and the New Jersey Literacy Association. Their changemaking energy continues to inspire our thoughts around literacy development.

Finally, we would like to thank our spouses for supporting our weekend writing workshop days and evenings where we disconnected to protect some writing time (in one case, escaping to a local coffee shop). We send our love to Tim, Bill, and Chris.

Contents

CHAPTER 1

Shared Literacy Leadership
Getting Involved on Behalf of All Readers and Writers

We're all in this really hard thing together. Sometimes we laugh,
sometimes we want to give up. But we're a team.
                                        —TARYN BENNETT

It is the beginning of a new school year as the literacy leadership team at Hatchery Hill
Elementary School reflect on last year's successes and challenges. As the principal of
the school, Mrs. Griffin experiences the same "butterflies-in-the-stomach" feeling that
accompanies the start of most new school years, but feels confident in knowing that the
school literacy team and district administration are there to support her. Hatchery Hill is
a warm and welcoming school community where everyone is involved and has a shared
mission and vision for helping each and every young reader and writer reach his or her
maximum potential. Within the school community, striving readers receive support from
Mrs. Rosenfeld, the literacy specialist and coach. District-level support is provided by
Mrs. Calabrese, a supervisor of curriculum and instruction who strongly believes in a
comprehensive approach to literacy instruction. Another feature that makes Hatchery Hill
unique is a teacher-leadership structure, in which informal leaders emerge through their focus
on best practices for teaching and learning. All voices in the school are heard and valued. A
new addition to the literacy team is Mrs. DeMarco, a lifelong learner who has been teaching
second grade for just a little more than 2 years. As the literacy team convenes in September,
Mrs. Griffin is excited that her team is balanced and includes a school principal, district-level
supervisor, reading specialist, and teacher. Wondering how to start the first meeting of the
year, Mrs. Griffin grabs a piece of chart paper and begins to write, "What is our 'WHY'?"
She begins to draft ideas for an inclusive tagline to support the school's mission and vision
statement. She thinks to herself, "How about: EVERY student is worth hatching"?

WHAT THE RESEARCH SAYS ABOUT SHARED LITERACY LEADERSHIP

Twenty-first-century literacy leadership is about a shared commitment toward improving student literacy performance: Shared leadership among stakeholders within and outside schools is necessary in order to actualize educational goals (Lewis-Spector & Jay, 2011). Literacy leadership cannot be shouldered by individuals, and, while there is plenty of research that demonstrates the leadership qualities needed by a principal, for example, for leading a school, studies that focus solely on shared efforts to impact literacy achievement are less common. However, we do know that literacy changemakers are often recognized for (1) having expertise in the foundations of literacy and in meeting the diverse needs of all learners, (2) being familiar with the theory and evolving research around new literacies, (3) sharing their beliefs and knowledge within the school community, and (4) finding creative ways to get their colleagues onboard to support this worthwhile work. When everyone works together and has a strong foundation in literacy best practices, great gains can be realized for students within a local school or district. This type of collaboration also ensures that the literacy aspects of the strategic plan of a school community stay on track, avoiding the top-down mandates that can often result from single individuals making decisions about language arts curriculum and instruction. Figure 1.1 highlights some of the key ingredients of a "literacy-strong" leadership team that are discussed in this chapter.

How to Find Your "Why"

In order to cultivate a school culture that embraces all students as readers and writers, it is important for all involved in this worthwhile work to have a shared belief about why the work is important. Shared literacy leadership means that everyone must get involved. Many books on school leadership emphasize the importance of getting your

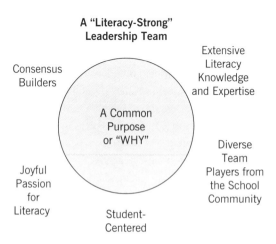

FIGURE 1.1. A framework for shared literacy leadership.

faculty and staff "turned on" to the work that lies ahead. In essence, all members of the school community should understand why they are needed and why their work will make the world a better place (Blanchard & Bowles, 1998). In *Move Your Bus: An Extraordinary New Approach to Accelerating Success in Work and Life,* Ron Clark (2015) describes the runners that you will find on your "bus" or within your school community: "These individuals are working as hard as possible, and they essentially carry the load of the bus. They come early or they stay late. They never complain, and they provide a positive spirit. Their work ethic is strong, and their attention to detail is spot on. They are the strongest members of the team, and they are the driving force behind the success of the organization" (p. 4). It is important to seek out the individuals who are committed to literacy teaching and learning. They are the faculty and staff members who are driven by a goal of professional excellence, which can be seen in their daily teaching, interactions with staff, and formal and informal leadership.

Lit 💡 Idea

Spend time listening and learning in your school community. Whether you are an administrator or teacher-leader, it is important to get a pulse for what is happening in your literacy community. Seek out volunteers and form a literacy team (see Figure 1.2). This team should consist of a diverse group of "runners" who are interested in supporting the literacy growth of the school. Team members may include, but are not limited to, administrators, teachers, reading specialists, reading coaches, parents, and child-study specialists. When forming the team, be sure that a majority of the members selected have a strong literacy content knowledge.

Dear K-8 ELA Teachers,

Happy New Year! We hope this email finds you warm and ready for the weekend.

In order to steer future efforts for professional development, we have developed a survey focused on our district's implementation of the K-8 reading and writing workshop model. Your responses to the survey questions will help to strengthen the literacy instruction provided to all learners in our district. Surveys for other content areas will be forthcoming.

Please complete this K-8 ELA survey https://goo.gl/forms/VVGys1c0hleAc1yV2 by Wednesday, January 10th.

In addition, the Office of Curriculum and Instruction is excited to announce the creation of district PD teams to explore new and innovative approaches to teaching and learning. Teams will be formed for Literacy, STEAM, Math, and Social Studies. Volunteer team members will attend PD events throughout the year and have future opportunities to share learning with colleagues. For additional details please email Dr. Ken Kunz at kunzk@middlesex.k12.nj.us.
One teacher from each school will be randomly chosen for a $10 Starbucks Gift Card. Providing an email address is optional, but will enter you into the raffle.

Thanks for your participation!
~Kate & Ken

FIGURE 1.2. A sample email invitation sent to faculty/staff for joining curricular teams.

In addition to forming a team, increasing staff engagement can also happen in more informal ways. For example, the #WhyITeach campaign on social media is an excellent example of teachers tapping into their "why" and telling their stories. Countless tweets with this hashtag can be found on Twitter as educators post reasons for why they are proud to be part of such a rewarding profession. No work is more rewarding and valuable than helping students find a joy and passion for reading and writing, while continuing to nurture and develop new skills and apply the new strategies they've learned. Teachers can use the template in Figure 1.3 to introduce students to who they are, and what inspires their teaching of reading and writing. Teachers can take a "shelfie," or selfie picture with a favorite book and post the #WhyITeach poster on their classroom doors to show students, parents, and local community members that literacy is an important part of our lives (see Figure 1.3).

Lit 💡 Idea

Reflect on whether or not your "why" includes a statement that shows a commitment to equity and social justice. Review your school or district mission and vision statement to determine if this commitment is explicitly stated. If not, engage your literacy team and school community in revisiting and revising your mission statement and tagline.

ELA Department: _____

#WHYITEACH

FIGURE 1.3. A template for teachers to reflect on their reasons for choosing to teach in English language arts.

Mixing Joy in with Your "Why"

As the title of this book suggests, it is our collective belief that now it is more impor-tant than ever for us to bring a joy for literacy teaching and learning back into schools and classrooms. Once everyone is turned on to the idea that promoting students' literacy development is worthwhile work, mixing in joy will reap great benefits. Throughout the book, our reference to the concept of bringing joy back into the classroom is based on the following belief: *Helping students realize their potential as readers and writers is an experience that will bring great pleasure and happiness to all of those involved.* According to Eckert (2016), "if I am not enjoying teaching, student learning will suf-fer. If I am bored, burned out, or beaten down, it is highly unlikely that my students will engage in vibrant learning. This is true for assessment, content, and classroom management—the three cornerstones of quality instruction" (p. 21). In essence, we have to look beyond the high-stakes testing and accountability that often take the joy out of the literacy classroom, and, while it would be naive to write off these powerful factors completely, teachers and literacy leaders are finding new ways to rise above the "noise" and challenges.

How to Build a Collaborative Team

No matter how strong the administration in a school may be, it is essential to build a collaborative team to create a positive and successful literacy environment where everyone embraces a common purpose and finds joy in helping students succeed. Your team will consist of a variety of stakeholders from the school community, and each member will play an important role in defining and sharing the vision, bring-ing staff members onboard, building excitement, providing professional development (PD), and mentoring teachers to achieve success. Once your team has been assembled, you will be amazed at the magic that can happen when you put them together in one room! Energy is contagious with leadership teams of dedicated teachers and staff members, and yours will be no different. But before you can start to celebrate your new, invigorated literacy environment, you need to assemble your team of change-makers.

Determining where to start can seem intimidating, but it may be simpler than you think. Deciding who your "runners" are is half the battle. Look around your school environment, and you'll find that nearly everyone you need is already beside you! There are also a wide variety of literacy experts and consultants you can bring into your schools to help guide the process, provide PD to fill gaps or raise awareness, and bring your school's literacy game to the next level. As we know, there is no one in a school with a better understanding of the students' and teachers' needs than the teachers themselves, and that's a great place to start. However, don't forget to look outside the teaching staff for potential literacy leaders. In *Coherence: The Right Drivers in Action for Schools, Districts, and Systems,* Michael Fullan and Joanne Quinn (2016) remind us of the importance of mindful collaboration: "Recognize that finding solu-tions to complex problems requires the intelligence and talents of everyone. Create a task team that is small but representative of the layers of the organization to strategize a plan and provide leadership" (p. 22). As you begin to form your collaborative team, consider potential members from various parts of the school community (see Figure 1.4). Keep in mind that it is not only acceptable to have dissenting voices or members with differing opinions on one collaborative team, it can also be necessary to push you in new and exciting directions. Be sure, however, that the people you choose to develop into literacy leaders will be willing to keep an open mind and work professionally alongside people with different beliefs.

In *Dare to Lead: Brave Work. Tough Conversations. Whole Hearts,* Brown (2018) refers to these folks as the "square squad." In essence, her concept suggests that if you were given a 1″ × 1″ square piece of paper, there are only so many people who will make the cut. They are not necessarily the literacy folks who agree with all of your ideas or those who "yes you to death." They are the individuals who challenge the status quo in productive ways, always looking to come up with new solutions to complex problems. They are innovative and flexible when it comes to change, and have a special way of dusting off their peers when it's needed, helping to keep the school on its feet, as opposed to basking in those moments where things seem to be "off balance." These team players are part of your "power posse," and will do anything to light and lift you up when it comes to this worthwhile work (Sincero, 2018). As you focus your energy on shared literacy leadership in a school community, unstoppable teams can be formed. At the same time, all teachers should be encouraged to think about who they can lean on to improve outcomes for kids.

Lit 💡 Idea

There is something energizing about being on a team that has shared beliefs for helping all students realize their potential as readers and writers. Building on your school's tagline, collectively come up with a team name that captures the essence of what your team is all about. For example, a playful, yet spirited, team name might look something like "Smells Like Literacy Team Spirit."

Hatchery Hill School

Where EVERY Student Is Worth Hatching

A sample school logo and tagline, demonstrating a shared belief that all students are valuable members of the learning community.

Team player	Unique contributions to the team
School principal	Building principals have an understanding of the instructional day schedule. They recognize the human capital within their building and how daily functions contribute to (or impede the progress of) educational initiatives. Although it is an added bonus to have a school leader that has expertise in an instructional area, not all of these leaders will identify as "literacy people" (yet). Their understanding of the schedule, finances, and school community needs are incredibly valuable.
Literacy coach/ reading specialist	The literacy coaches and reading specialists likely have advanced degrees, training, and professional development when it comes to a highly specialized area such as literacy. These folks bring a passion to the team because they recognize that literacy opens doors and worlds of possibilities for learners. Invest in their talents.
District supervisor or administrator	District-level administrators play a unique role in that they serve as ambassadors between every school's needs and what's outlined in the district's strategic plan (a cluster of what the district, community, and often-changing local boards of education value). Leaders in this role often have access to a plethora of resources and can support literacy initiatives.
Data specialist	As school leaders, we have to take an *honest* look at our data. We all know that data can be used to tell a story, and this story can be manipulated on the basis of how it's presented. For example, school performance reports may show that all targets are met for literacy achievement, but a deeper look at the data suggests that marginalized populations are not meeting targets. If your district does not have a data specialist, consult with an expert who can help point out trends over time and evolving needs. Professional development and professional learning that is steered by fads or spur-of-the-moment hunches or trends are bound to kill the spirit of the faculty and staff.
Teacher	Research confirms that teachers are the number one in-school influence on student achievement, and nothing beats having a respected and quality teacher on a literacy team. Including teachers from different programs and backgrounds is also helpful. Teachers will have expertise in different areas, depending on their courses of study, certifications, and advanced degrees and/or training. Get to know the teachers to find out what they've accomplished, what they've studied, and what drives their passion for teaching and learning.
Librarian or media specialist	Some of the latest controversies involve ongoing debates as to whether or not having high-quality classroom libraries replaces the need for media specialists and school libraries. It is our unified stance that they work in tandem. Countless articles and resources published by the American Association of School Librarians demonstrate how a joyful librarian and a well-stocked library can transform the literacy culture of a school. In every high-achieving school we have worked in, the library has served as a hub, and even the "heartbeat" of the school.
Support staff	In *Breaking Through the Language Arts Block: Organizing and Managing the Exemplary Literacy Day* (Morrow et al., 2018), it is argued that language can be used to create a literacy community in the classroom. This same language broadly impacts the school community as a whole. Involve staff members who recognize (or are open to the fact) that literacy development, within the school context, occurs the moment students leave their homes to attend school until the moment they go home. This includes, but is not limited to, administrative assistants, teachers' aides, custodial staff, cafeteria workers, and school crossing guards. Ask yourself: Who will support our literacy initiatives A.M. to P.M.?

(continued)

FIGURE 1.4. An incomplete list of potential literacy team players.

Team player	Unique contributions to the team
Parent	Parents all want the best for their children. If you are able to identify one, or even a few key parents to be part of the literacy team, you will have insight into messages about the school's progress based on a variety of social media representations and talk between parents. Parents are always invested in their local schools and have a vested interest in these schools serving the needs of their children. The story we imagine may not always be the story being told.
Board of education member	These individuals have been elected to represent the community regarding the management of the public schools. Connect with board members who have a shared interest in literacy. In order to do this, you have to attend board functions (e.g., board meetings, curriculum committee meetings). Find the board member who shares a wide smile when curriculum is updated to reflect the diversity of the children attending the district's schools. Embrace the board member who smiles from ear to ear when discussing that books are making their way into homes and reaching the hands of readers of all ages.
College/university literacy consultant	It is well known that every school and district has a story that is being written (voluntarily or involuntarily). Partner with a local college or university literacy consultant to take charge of your literacy story. Even with the smallest amount of federal, state, or local funds, our team has witnessed literacy transformations in myriad ways. Take advantage of the research and scholarship that often exist not far from the city limits of where you teach and learn.

FIGURE 1.4. *(continued)*

A bulletin board space allows for "staff shout-outs," building a collaborative culture in the school.

How to Seek Out the Connected Literacy Leaders

When seeking out connected literacy leaders in our school communities one should consider the words of Brown (2018): "a leader is someone who holds herself or himself accountable for finding potential in people and processes." Therefore, as literacy changemakers we must be accountable for finding the potential in those assigned to our charge. Seeking out these individuals should not be a simple formality, or a matter of choosing favorites or familiar colleagues, and most definitely should not involve nepotism. As the leader of a school community, caution and care should be dedicated to seeking out those who are committed to 21st-century learning, contemporary best practices, and virtual professional learning networks (PLNs). We must keep an eye out for the individuals who are engaged in professional development long after the dismissal bell has rung.

True literacy leaders can often be overlooked and be hidden in plain sight. They may be outliers, for example, implementing practices unfamiliar to some of the in-house colleagues. Where are these other forward-thinking educators? Many are found sharing virtual PLNs or attending unconferences, such as Global EdCamps,

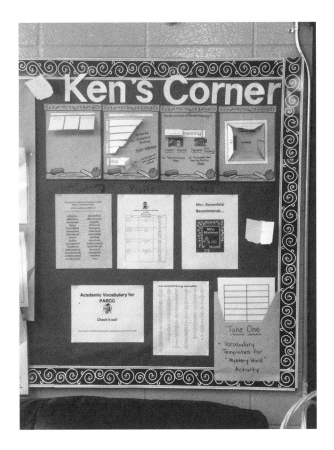

A bulletin board space in the faculty room of a school provides an area where teachers can access literacy resources from the literacy specialist/coach.

and collaborative events taking place on weekends. Twitter is one platform where countless educators connect daily with colleagues in their favorite PLNs. They connect to share ideas, to learn from one another, and to improve their craft and practice. Imagine the wealth of knowledge shared across social media from the highest level administrators to preservice educators. Then, picture the individuals who return to their school communities full of newfound passion, insight, and wisdom. They are the literacy leaders who have the fuel to fire up literacy initiatives. Ask yourself: Are any of the folks described here hidden in plain sight in your school community? If so, it is worth every effort to get these changemakers on the team!

Lit 💡 Idea

After professional development days or literacy workshops have taken place, keep an eye out for the leaders who have returned fully ignited and equipped to lead change and be part of a greater literacy movement. They may be walking and talking missed opportunities. Take a moment to canvass these hidden jewels within your school communities. Identify the literacy areas in need of attention where these leaders can take action and get involved.

Emphasizing a Core Mission and Values for Literacy

Once a strong team is established, it may still take time for individuals to articulate a core literacy mission and literacy values for the school community. Consider the challenge posed in the following anecdote:

> After partnering with a local university's literacy center, Mrs. Griffin is excited to have some additional support in her school, as fresh and new ideas for comprehensive literacy instruction are shared with her literacy team. Teachers appear to be embracing the components of an exemplary literacy day and excited to begin making changes to their instruction with embedded support from coaches. One influential member of the team, however, remains unsure about the "why" behind the literacy work that the school is pursuing. He asks, "If our scores are so low, can't we just have the students read at home and not in school, so that the teachers can teach when the kids are in class?"

It is evident that, at times, literacy team members or stakeholders in a local community will question the decisions that teachers and administrators make when it comes to teaching and learning. If you are familiar with the work of the "book whisperer," Donalyn Miller, you may realize that the time is ripe for the literacy team to declare, "We've got research, yes we do! We've got research, how about you?" A core literacy mission and literacy instruction values should be based on key findings in the research. For example, Allington (2002) found that time spent reading in school is one of the major factors that define effective literacy instruction. He warns that when "stuff" dominates reading instruction, warning flags should go up, and that classrooms with high levels of student literacy achievement include opportunities for more guided reading, independent reading, and reading in the content areas. According to the International Literacy Association (ILA; 2018b), over 781 million people worldwide still cannot read and write. We also know that if a child is not on grade level by the end of third grade, he or she has less than a 10% chance of ever making it to grade level in the future. A collaborative literacy team must reference the research and present a call to action that brings all stakeholders on board.

Lit 💡 Idea

Recognize the difference between a literacy core mission and values. When drafting a literacy core mission, the literacy team should reflect on what the school community is actually going to *do* for all readers and writers. The values should be a statement of what the local school community *aspires to do* for all readers and writers.

BEGIN WITH THE END IN MIND: WELCOME TO THE EXEMPLARY LITERACY DAY

In *Breaking Through the Language Arts Block: Organizing and Managing the Exemplary Literacy Day* (Morrow, Kunz, & Hall, 2018), we began our work by introducing the literacy community to our new way of thinking about moving beyond what is traditionally referred to as the "reading block." Instead, our work with colleagues at Rutgers University led us to embrace the idea of a comprehensive literacy day over a "balanced" program with pieced-together components of literacy instruction. In essence, we advocate for a literacy day in which readers and writers engage in authentic and relevant literacy experiences across the school day and beyond the reading classroom. Morrow et al. (2018) state, "It is important to understand that the exemplary literacy day is not a prepackaged program. Instead, it is a compilation of best practices that will allow teachers to use data and professional judgment to become experts in their craft. Research has proven that there is no program or material that is best for all children" (p. 2).

Because it is our belief that literacy changemaking is not limited to early childhood and elementary schools, two formats for an exemplary or ideal, literacy day are outlined (see Figures 1.5 and 1.6). While the K–6 exemplary literacy day is dissected in detail in *Breaking through the Language Arts Block: Organizing and Managing the Exemplary Literacy Day,* it is our belief that a core part of being a literacy changemaker is embracing the nature of literacy instruction and the possibilities that exist when decisions not to use purchased programs are made. Each outlined exemplary literacy day can be orchestrated through authentic lesson and unit design or by adapting resources provided by local schools and districts.

Do-Now or Think-Now (10–15 minutes)
Upon arriving at school, students should . . .
- Engage in an immediate independent or partner activity in reading or writing that sets the tone for the rest of the day.
- Practice skills and strategies previously taught and prepare for the day's lessons.
- Partner read/write or independently read/write.
- Contribute to writing journal entries.
- Take a partner on a tour of his or her reading or writing journal.

Vocabulary Meeting (15–20 minutes)
- Students participate in an activity centered on a vocabulary-enriched message.
- Students collaborate to deepen their understanding of word meanings.
- Utilize a vocabulary word wall in the classroom to reinforce word meanings.

Reading Comprehension Workshop (time varies, 30–60 minutes)
- Time may be spent engaging the students in a read-aloud, during which the teacher will utilize questioning and think-aloud techniques.
- Students engage in a comprehension-focused mini-lesson, in which strategies and skills are taught to help students master grade-appropriate comprehension skills.
- Time is set aside for independent/partner practice concentrating on the strategies and skills taught.
- The teacher confers with readers.
- The teacher and students participate in a group share.

Guided Reading, Strategy Groups, and Literacy Work Stations (minimum of two rotations of 15–20 minutes each)
- For guided reading, teachers meet with small, homogeneous groups of no more than six students to explicitly teach strategies and reinforce skills as needed.
- With strategy groups, teachers meet with small, heterogeneous groups of no more than six students who share a common need for strategy or skill instruction.
- Students can move through literacy work stations to practice strategies and skills previously taught. An accountability assignment should be included at each literacy station; however, the teacher may choose to emphasize one accountability assignment in particular.
- When students reach a maximum 40-minute stamina for independent reading, teachers may choose to utilize literacy work stations only when needed.
- Common literacy work stations include listening (comprehension), word work (vocabulary and spelling), writing (independent or partner), library (independent or partner), and technology (skill-based programs).

Word-Work Session (15–20 minutes, but varies according to different approaches used)
- Teachers provide explicit instruction in phonemic awareness (for early and emergent readers) *or* phonics/decoding (for emergent, transitional, and fluent readers).
- Students often engage in word sorts, word building, and word games.
- Programs vary according to school districts.

Writing Workshop (time varies, 30–60 minutes)
- Students engage in a writing-focused mini-lesson in which strategies are taught to help them master grade-appropriate writing skills.
- Time is set aside for independent/partner practice concentrating on the strategies and skills taught.
- The teacher confers with writers.
- The teacher and students participate in a group share.

Interdisciplinary Project-Based Instruction (IPBI) (time varies)
- IPBI is a student-interest-based project that crosses disciplines.
- Long-term activities include research and the creation and completion of a project that demonstrates student learning.

(continued)

FIGURE 1.5. Sample exemplary elementary literacy day.

- IPBI may also include connections to iSTEAM (integrated Science, Technology, Engineering, Arts, and Mathematics).
- Reading and writing skills are embedded throughout the project.

Wrap-Up (5 minutes)
At the end of each school day, conclude on a positive note by saying to the students:
- "What did you learn today in reading and writing that is most important to you?"
- "You can choose to read a poem, riddle, joke, or short story, or to sing a song."

FIGURE 1.5. *(continued)*

For schools that utilize a block schedule, the time spent on each component can be doubled or adjusted based on the needs of the students.

Do-Now or Think-Now (10–15 minutes)
Upon arriving at school, students should . . .
- Engage in an immediate independent or partner activity in reading or writing that sets the tone for the rest of the day.
- Squeeze juicy vocabulary words to create lists of synonyms/antonyms, student-friendly definitions, graphic or illustrated representations, lists of words based on an analysis of word roots or meaningful word parts.
- Practice the skills and strategies previously taught and prepare for the day's lessons.
- Partner read/write or independently read/write.
- Contribute to writing journal entries.
- Take a partner on a tour of his or her reading or writing journal.

Optional: When time is scarce, consider rotating the use of the Reading Comprehension Workshop and the Writing Workshop.

Reading Comprehension Workshop (time varies, 30 minutes)
- Time may be spent engaging the students in a read-aloud, in which the teacher will utilize questioning and think-aloud techniques.
- Students engage in a comprehension-focused mini-lesson in which strategies and skills are taught to help students master grade-appropriate comprehension skills.
- Time is set aside for independent/partner practice concentrating on the strategies and skills taught.
- Students may spend time collaborating in inquiry literature circles or book clubs.
- The teacher confers with readers.
- The teacher and students participate in a group share.

Writing Workshop (time varies, 30 minutes)
- Students engage in a writing-focused mini-lesson in which strategies are taught to help them master grade-appropriate writing skills.
- Time is set aside for independent/partner practice concentrating on the strategies and skills taught.
- The teacher confers with writers.
- The teacher and students participate in a group share.

Wrap-Up (5 minutes)
- At the end of each school day, end on a positive note by asking the students:
- "How does your independent reading today contribute to your reading life?"
- "What reading and writing skills or strategies have you been working on?"

FIGURE 1.6. Sample exemplary middle and high school literacy day.

Lit 💡 Idea

Beginning with the end in mind can have a promising impact if teachers and building leaders are able to witness best practices in action. When it comes to the implementation of an exemplary literacy day, consider reflecting on the following question: "Which are the schools and districts to watch?" Scheduling a visit to another school allows you to reimagine what literacy instruction could look like in your school. To avoid information overload, insist that each team visitor look at the school environment through a different lens.

TAKE THE TIME TO BUILD CONSENSUS

All of the research and experience of our own point to the fact that consensus within the group when making decisions is truly important. But when we speak of consensus, what exactly do we mean? Consensus does not mean that all members of the group have reached 100% agreement about a course of action. It does, however, mean that all stakeholders have gone through a process that has allowed them a voice in the decision making, and that the decision is something all parties "can live with." It is generally agreed that the principles of consensus building include that it is:

- inclusive, in that as many stakeholders are involved in the discussions as possible;
- participatory, because everyone is given a chance to contribute;
- collaborative, as the group modifies the proposal to address individual needs, but no one has individual ownership;
- agreement seeking, because the goal is to find as much agreement as possible; and
- cooperative, in that the good of the group is foremost in the minds of stakeholders.

Building consensus is a multistep process, and all members of the group need to understand its ultimate goal. It is helpful, also, to bring food to meetings. While having food may seem like a small gesture, it can have a big impact when the group is "hitting the wall" and needs just a small boost to regain momentum. A highly successful consensus-building superintendent we know always carried a "chocolate salad" to team meetings. This, of course, was a large crystal bowl filled to the brim with all kinds of chocolate "fun-size" candy bars and tossed with salad tongs. For many people, chocolate = joy. We have witnessed several times when this kind of treat helped to save the day.

The steps in the consensus-building process include:

- discussion,
- identification of the proposal,
- identification of remaining concerns,

- collaborative modification of the proposal to address concerns,
- assessment of the degree of support for the proposal, and
- finalization of the decision or a return to the step that addresses remaining concerns.

There are several reasons to use this process, because the goals include concepts that make it most productive for school groups. The process also results in decisions that are more likely to:

- be better for the group, since they include input from each stakeholder;
- allow for better implementation, due to the degree of agreement by all parties; and
- contribute to better group relationships because of the cooperative group atmosphere.

Would it be simpler for a central office administrator or principal to create a mission statement and an action plan and hand it down to teachers, parents, and students? Quite possibly, yes. The trouble with this model is that we have all seen it fail so many times. Without the buy-in of major stakeholders and the commitment achieved through consensus, even the strongest initiatives will often fail to take hold.

CONCLUSION

In this chapter, we present a case for shared literacy leadership and the importance of having a team joyfully engaged in collaborating around a shared purpose (why) for impacting readers and writers across diverse school contexts. We combine the research (what) with the practice (how), while reintroducing the exemplary literacy day and the components of comprehensive literacy instruction. "Lit Ideas" for success in classrooms and schools are suggested, and opportunities for advocating for social justice and equity are introduced. The reader is introduced to literacy changemakers and vignettes representing real leaders and decision makers in the field. Now, it is time for an aspiring literacy changemaker to stop, think, and take action.

Stop, Think, and Take Action

Based on the ideas presented in this chapter on shared literacy leadership, take time to consider the ways in which you might get everyone involved to support readers and writers in your local school community. Reflect on the following:

If your role is that of a . . .

- **Classroom teacher** or **teacher-leader**—Consider the impact that you have in your classroom and local school community. What is one idea from the chapter that you could put into practice? Think of one or two colleagues who might be willing to join you.
- **Literacy specialist** or **literacy coach**—What are the benefits of forming a literacy team

in your school? If you already have a team formed, how might you engage teachers in reflecting on the exemplary literacy day?

- **School administrator** or **school-level leader**—What are some ways in which you will communicate your "why" with key stakeholders? How will you spotlight your literacy mission and core values?

- **District administrator** or **district-level leader**—We live in a world where data seem plentiful. Moving beyond simply documenting literacy successes and challenges, consider a forum for having an honest conversation about student achievement. Ask yourself, "Which students in the school community need your attention now more than ever?"

- **Professional developer**—Consider how you can support the decisions that the educational professionals in the schools where you work have made. Plan two to three steps to foster a sense of shared leadership in the school community.

CHAPTER 2

Engaging and Joyful Literacy Leadership

The teacher has a duty to engage, to create romance that can transform apathy into interest and, if a teacher does her job well, a sort of transference of enthusiasm from teacher to student takes place.

> —RAYMOND TELLER (of Penn & Teller)

The literacy leadership team at Hatchery Hill has come to a consensus that every child is indeed worth hatching, that literacy is our school's priority, and that every child has a fundamental right to read. Mrs. Griffin believes that, while there is a tremendous amount of pressure and responsibility related to these goals, the faculty and staff in her school must stay on track with true engagement and joy. She is sensitive to the idea that teachers need to love coming to work, and hopes that this enthusiasm will create classrooms where readers strive to reach their true potential. Mrs. Rosenfeld adds, "I believe that my role as a coach can support teachers in this work, and that relationship building is important. I wonder if we can start by having our teachers reflect on why we love the work that we do." Mrs. Calabrese suggests that this work is a perfect opportunity to involve the Board of Education Curriculum Committee and maps out a date on the calendar to invite the literacy leadership team to the next board meeting when that committee will meet. The principal decides that her next faculty meeting will be less about the mundane, with time set aside for Mrs. DeMarco to facilitate an activity on joyful literacy leadership based on "I Wish You Knew . . ." from *Kids Deserve It* (Nesloney & Welcome, 2016).

WHAT THE RESEARCH SAYS ABOUT ENGAGEMENT AND JOY

In Chapter 1, we asserted that helping students realize their potential as readers and writers is an experience that will bring great pleasure and happiness to all of those involved. Research, especially by John Guthrie, suggests that there is a positive relationship between motivation for reading and a student's literacy achievement. He states that "'skill' and 'will' go hand in hand" (in O'Donnell, 2017). The most joyful parts of teaching often take place when we witness a student's individual "Aha!" moment. Those moments are more likely to occur when we have recognized and made room in our classrooms for the three motivations that drive student reading: interest, dedication, and confidence. When a child demonstrates intrinsic interest, she reads because she enjoys it. Dedication causes her to read because she believes it to be important. Confidence, perhaps the strongest motivator, happens when she believes she has the capacity to read and understand.

As teachers, we can encourage motivation by ensuring that we allow our students to experience:

- choice (of materials, partners, etc.),
- collaboration (with peers),
- relevance to their world (making connections),
- periodic positive feedback, and
- teacher support when necessary.

"Readerly Lives"

Jane Losinger, a supervisor of language arts in New Jersey, reminds us of her belief that we are shortchanging reading engagement. With the best intentions, teachers in this era of rigorous standards have been diving headfirst into close reading for author's purpose, analyzing the structure of texts, and synthesizing information from multiple sources, completely overlooking the importance of truly developing students into passionate, devoted readers. Jane explains, "the irony is that if we spend more time nurturing our students' 'readerly lives,' the rest of our teaching will be easier." Our team believes that it will be easier and more productive, and understands that while we respect grit as an important habit of mind, we should not harness grit at the expense of fostering joy. Let's start by banking one-on-one time with our students to get to know their academic and personal goals and to support their "readerly lives."

Lit 💡 Idea

Within the first 6 weeks of school, bank one-on-one time with your learners in the classroom by scheduling mini-appointments. Ask students about their hopes, dreams, and aspirations:

- "What is an academic goal that you have for this school year?"
- "What is a social goal that you have for this school year?"
- "Is there anything else I need to know to help you become a stronger reader or writer?"

Keep notes of the conference so that you can refer back to them when it is time for a follow-up visit. According to research, taking time to get to know your learners in this way can increase student engagement in classrooms by 33% and decrease misbehavior by 75% (Terada, 2019).

Teacher Self-Efficacy

While teacher self-efficacy is not a new idea, only recently have we recognized the strength of the correlation between collective teacher efficacy and student achievement. John Hattie now ranks the collective belief of teachers in their ability to positively affect students as the number one influence related to student achievement. It is important to note that this is not merely a growth mindset belief, but "when you fundamentally believe you can make a difference and then you feed it with the evidence that you are, that is dramatically powerful" (Visible Learning, 2018).

We have long known that the biggest variable in the classroom is not the children, their socioeconomic background, or the program used to instruct them, but the teacher. One teacher's belief that she can affect change and growth in her students (her own beliefs in self-efficacy) over the course of the year can make a huge difference in the academic achievement of the children in her classroom. When all teachers in a school believe that they are what motivates learning in their students, the combined effect is exponentially stronger. Teachers who work in such an atmosphere experience the joy of teaching over and over again.

Literacy Engagement and Joy

Consider five key ingredients for bringing joy back into focus when it comes to literacy learning in your school or district (Figure 2.1). Grouped into five key areas, these ingredients provide a lens through which we can maintain a focus on encouraging love of learning and literacy, ensuring that joy is a contagious and continuous part of the school day for both students *and* teachers!

Willis (2007) adds that when the fun stops, the learning will stop too. Lessons from neuroscience teach us that the brain learns best when the environment is stimulating and anxiety is low. Five tips for classroom teachers are the following:

1. Keep it relevant.
2. Give periodic breaks.
3. Create positive associations.
4. Prioritize information.
5. Allow time for independent discovery.

"I Wish You Knew" Activity

There is great potential to grow a love of reading in students when they develop high levels of trust in their teachers. Students who trust their teachers enough to share with them the details of their lives often provide important insights that help not only create stronger connections, but also opportunities to understand their interests, motivations, and hurdles. One way of connecting with students is through a low-pressure activity like that featured in "I Wish You Knew . . ." from *Kids Deserve It* (Nesloney & Welcome, 2016). This activity can be completed in journals, private Google Classroom responses, or on slips of paper. Each student writes down something she wishes the teacher knew about her. It could be as simple as a favorite activity ("I wish my

As literacy changemakers, we must spend time focusing our energy on . . .	This impacts our classroom and school community because all of our readers and writers will . . .
1. Building trust	• believe in their abilities to succeed. • embrace a growth mindset of "I'm not where I need to be as a reader/writer . . . *yet.*" • recognize that all teachers and role models in the school community are there to provide just the right dose of support.
2. Taking risks	• benefit from changes that we make to ensure that our literacy instruction is not just balanced, but comprehensive. • be exposed to the many new literacies centered around reading, writing, speaking, listening, and viewing skills. • be future-ready learners who think critically.
3. Promoting inquiry through wonder	• question current existing thinking and potential misconceptions. • engage to explore and find answers to new questions and emerging curiosities. • develop a strategy for testing and finding solutions to existing problems.
4. Prioritizing goals	• set goals related to reading and writing instruction. • see beyond reading as a "level" and understand the gradual steps that can be taken to make progress in learning. • grow because literacy changemakers are taking a fresh and honest look at the many forms of data available.
5. Finding entertainment in all that exists around us	• hold on to a passion for reading and writing that all too often diminishes in the upper grades. • appreciate the joy that is learning. • share relevant and authentic literacy experiences with classmates, relatives, and various audiences.

FIGURE 2.1. Five key ingredients for bringing joy back into literacy learning.

teacher knew I love to draw but never share my artwork") and as complex as a changing family dynamic ("I wish my teacher knew my parents are separating, and I sleep on the floor at my aunt's house").

This activity is beautiful in its simplicity and potential. Students are in no way required to share anything more serious than what they had for lunch that day, but there is an opportunity for those who need and want help to open up their worlds in a low-pressure, casual manner. So, what does the teacher have to gain from this activity? Aside from connections with students, she or he can help students find novels or articles that correspond to their interests, help them identify topics on which they may want to focus in their reading or writing, or recognize students who are reaching out for help, be it emotional or academic.

Another crucial outcome of this activity is the potential for the teacher to address her own bias, conscious or subconscious, by finding out who her students are based on what they share. This is especially true of students who are at risk or from minority cultures, including English as a second language (ESL) and immigrant students. In an inspiring TED Talk (2009), *The Danger of a Single Story,* Chimamanda Ngozi Adichie shares the ways that her classmates and professors characterized her based on her status as an immigrant from Africa. Their expectation that she lived a poor, rural life spent dancing to tribal music would certainly be problematic when trying to connect with her as a student who, in her real life, preferred Mariah Carey and grew up with servants in her home. Clearing up any misconceptions can only lead to increased trust between the teacher and her students, creating a more positive and joyful learning environment for all.

This activity tells students that they are important, that they are valued, and they are heard. And, it is so much easier to help our students recognize and spark joy when they feel understood, appreciated, and respected.

"I Wish You Knew . . . : I'm Building a Reading Stack"

We can also build a joy for reading and writing in our schools by encouraging all faculty and staff members to share their (grade-appropriate) reading interests with students and the school community at large. One of the latest initiatives of the National Council of Teachers of English (NCTE) involves helping teachers and school community leaders identify themselves as readers. NCTE asserts that "the right book in the right hands can transform a life." Using social media, NCTE promotes the #buildyourstack initiative to share joy for reading voluminously (Sibberson, 2018). Recently, we began to adapt this vision to school settings, encouraging readers to show not only what they are reading now, but also what joy for reading looms after the first text is completed.

Lit 💡 Idea

Provide all of the teachers and staff with a plastic sheet protector and the #buildyourstack template (below) at a faculty meeting or individual department meetings. Begin by sharing a book or article that you have recently read and were excited about. Explain how Right Number 5 of the International Literacy Association's Rights to Read affected your decision to read for pleasure. Encourage your school community members to share what they are currently reading for pleasure and what's next up on their reading stacks. For staff members who may be hesitant about sharing, assist in writing a new story. Be a "book whisperer," and help connect participants with a mystery book that can be traded based on interest.

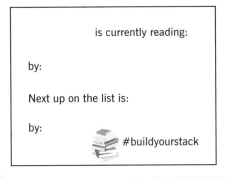

is currently reading:

by:

Next up on the list is:

by:

#buildyourstack

A #buildyourstack template for fostering a school culture in which current and future book choices are shared.

PROTECTING CHILDREN'S RIGHTS TO READ

As literacy leaders, we recognize that making personal connections within a school community and personally identifying as a reader or writer can bring joy back into focus in schools. When we reflect on our "why," we must also recognize that the work that we are doing is a basic fundamental human right that holds the potential to empower (or diminish) the opportunities one is provided for college and career readiness. Launched in 2018, ILA (2019) sparked a campaign around Children's Rights to Read, a list of 10 statements that summarize what our students fundamentally deserve with respect to literacy (see Figure 2.2). In addition to pledging and enacting these rights in our classrooms and schools, it is our belief that these rights can bring collective joy to a community of literacy leaders. Consider Right Number 4, for example. If a school is committed to ensuring that students are represented in the curriculum, a number of steps can be taken to (1) celebrate a commitment to such efforts and (2) transform classroom and school libraries. Literacy leaders can work together to audit the curriculum to determine if diverse languages, cultures, families, and identities (e.g., LGBTQ+) are represented. Collective efforts can be made to introduce new children's books, mentor texts, and read-alouds.

These rights can be used in imaginative ways, but it all begins with exposure. At a faculty meeting or teacher inservice, literacy team players should collectively discuss what rights are being advocated for strongly (this is what we do really well), and what rights need improvement (this deserves a second glance). At the district level, it is important for boards of education to adopt formal resolutions around these rights, showing community members that literacy is an important cornerstone for learning.

---

1. Children have the basic human right to read.

2. Children have the right to access texts in print and digital formats.

3. Children have the right to choose what they read.

4. Children have the right to read texts that mirror their experiences and languages, provide windows into the lives of others, and open doors into our diverse world.

5. Children have the right to read for pleasure.

6. Children have the right to supportive reading environments with knowledgeable literacy partners.

7. Children have the right to extended time set aside for reading.

8. Children have the right to share what they learn through reading by collaborating with others locally and globally.

9. Children have the right to read as a springboard for other forms of communication, such as writing, speaking, and visually representing.

10. Children have the right to benefit from the financial and material resources of governments, agencies, and organizations that support reading and reading instruction.

FIGURE 2.2. A look at ILA's Children's Rights to Read.

Lit 💡 Idea

Providing books to classrooms is not a "one-shot deal." Instead, we should be looking at the ever-changing dynamics in our school communities and staying on top of the latest releases in literature to keep literacy exciting in our schools. When new books are purchased for classroom and school libraries, make it a big celebration and invite the students to participate. Across grade levels, students experience joy unboxing new collections of books and checking out potential titles that are unfamiliar. Share this story publicly as well through pictures, social media, websites, and more.

EXAMPLES OF SPARKING A SCHOOLWIDE JOY FOR THE WORK AHEAD

Throughout the rest of the chapter, we reflect on some examples of how to spark a schoolwide joy for the literacy work ahead. While this is not an exhaustive list of ideas, the descriptions provide a glimpse into school communities where teachers love coming to work, students love coming to school, and literacy achievements are celebrated daily.

Beyond *Read Across America* Week: Schoolwide Read-Aloud Initiatives

There are wonderful schoolwide initiatives happening everywhere. In a small town in New Jersey, a potential principal asked his literacy coach for help in setting up a "Book Buddies" program as part of his internship. Together the coach and the teacher sought out students in kindergarten and first grade who were not being read to at home and matched them up with eighth graders who wished to complete community service hours by reading to younger children. The older students were given training in how to conduct an interactive read-aloud and how to encourage young children. Armed with well-written and beautifully illustrated picture books, they spent their "work" period (the last period of their day) reading aloud, and talking, drawing, and writing about the books they shared. Eventually, the younger children took over some of the reading as the semester went by. When asked to write about their experiences, the older students responded that they felt great about their contributions, and the younger children told the adults that they had learned that reading was a lifelong skill and one that they could accomplish and cherish themselves.

Fostering a "Word Nerd" Culture

It is not difficult to foster a culture that values words and their acquisition. At the root of this concept is the idea of word consciousness, meaning that teachers and students are eager to learn and use new words. When teachers stress beautiful or highly descriptive language as they are reading aloud, when they pause and say to children, "Did you hear that word? What could it mean? Why did the author choose to use that particular word? Let's write it down and check it out later," they are fostering word consciousness. As they go on to teach several words each week explicitly, they are developing "word nerds" in the classroom. As words are displayed, referred to, discussed, and argued over, it becomes second nature for children to search for the perfect word as they write. They will have learned the value of vocabulary, which is incredibly helpful in comprehension.

If, however, we want the concept of word nerds to be developed as a part of a schoolwide shift in culture, leadership needs to be involved. Often a principal (or a coach) will announce the word of the week and its definition via the loudspeaker on Mondays, and have classes submit synonyms, antonyms, and spectacular sentences during the week. In this way, students become word conscious painlessly. You will learn more strategies related to this idea throughout the rest of the book.

Sharing an Excitement for Choice Reading

As educators, we all know the value of independent reading, both in school and at home. There are lots of ways to make independent reading a joyful time. First, children need to know that they may choose their own books. Choice is a huge motivator, and students will work harder to read and comprehend a book on a subject they have chosen.

This year, at a back-to-school night, the school's literacy coach decided to create a video in which parents were asked to read to or with their children even more than they had been doing. She enlisted the aid of the highly effective technology teacher, who helped her create a 2-minute video to be shown in every classroom that evening. In the video she reminded everyone that the way to become a better reader was to increase the volume of our reading and that parents could help by continuing to read nightly to their children. The next morning a teacher reported to the coach that a parent had asked her, "Do you think this literacy coach could help my son want to read? He hates reading."

The teacher and the coach put their heads together and came up with a series of lessons that could help struggling and disaffected readers. The coach explained, "All of the current research stresses how important *volume* is in elementary school reading. If we hope to increase the volume that our students are reading, the best way to go about it is to convince children that reading is the wonderful pastime that it is. The only way to accomplish this—to create people who love to read—is to find each of our students a book that speaks to them so strongly that they *want* to continue reading it. To that end, in each classroom I visited today I conducted a read-aloud of *Miss Malarkey Leaves No Reader Behind* (Finchler & O'Malley, 2010). The teachers and I then helped each student fill out an interest inventory. With these inventories in hand the next day, the classroom teacher showed her children how to locate the digital card catalog for the school library. Once students determined the topic in which they were most interested, they entered their topic and, like magic, they were rewarded by seeing all of the books contained in the library on that topic pop up. We discussed how to locate a book in the library using the call numbers, had students write down the call numbers and the book titles, and took students to the library to find their books."

We followed up on these children after all students in grades 2, 3, and 4 had completed these lessons. It took a couple of weeks (okay, it took a month or 2) but now, as the coach walks around the school, she is met by cries of "Hey, Miss Malarkey, have you read this great book? It's the best!" Talk about bringing joy back into teaching—this coach is walking on air! The child's teacher is thrilled to welcome into her room a group of children who have begun to value reading, and the mom of the child who hated to read wrote notes to the school, expressing the joy with which she watches her son read at home.

In a second-grade classroom where two children are in charge of the (large) classroom library each week, a couple of girls recently decided that they would highlight books that hadn't been checked out for a while. In order to spark interest among their classmates, their literacy coach showed them samples of the "staff picks" from her local bookstore. She helped them determine what should be in a quick book review, they wrote a few and posted them in the library, and, to their delight, those books are now flying off the shelves! The next week's "librarians" decided to write staff picks for books they loved, and the same thing happened. The entire class is now learning how to give book talks and create book trailers so that they can share their favorite books with classmates. The teacher in this room had injected her room with joy.

Newton's "Law of Literacy"

If we can, for a moment, stretch Newton's laws of motion and apply them to literacy, we can state that the energy we put out is the energy we get back. That is, the more time, effort, and energy we pour into our work (backed, of course, by research, and evidenced by measures of student achievement) the greater our return will be.

We all know educators who absolutely love what they do. Hopefully that includes you! When you see them in the hallway, they have a certain energy that is almost contagious. They are excited about their learning environments, their students, their lessons, their ideas, and their colleagues. Practically without fail, these teachers have students who genuinely enjoy their school days and are excited about learning. And the outcome of all of this positive energy? The students work hard and grow—socially, emotionally, and academically. There will obviously be struggling learners, but they are often different. These struggling learners put in the effort, they demonstrate perseverance, and they have a strong work ethic. They take pride in their work. Naturally, some of their achievement could be a result of their character, but often it is a result of their environment, which is carefully curated by their conscientious teachers.

Here you have Newton's law of literacy! Teachers who are excited about reading help students become excited readers. Have you heard a teacher read a novel to her students with expression and engagement that draws you in, even as an adult? What you likely don't see after this lesson include the students who intentionally seek out this author for the rest of the year because he or she has captured their interest, or the student who has never liked to read but whose interest was piqued by this particular novel. Perhaps you were this teacher yourself. If so, bravo! You've been using Newton's law of literacy to instill a love of reading in your students.

Celebrating Small Wins: Keeping the Momentum Going

The big question facing every coach and school leader is: even in my absence will this initiative continue? And the answer lies in the degree to which we have had an impact on the school culture. As coaches, we can visit teachers in August, as they work on their classroom environments, to remind them of the school's commitment to a "culture of literacy," and the fact that it requires a wonderfully attractive and enticing library corner. We can help by working to sort books, to order carpets, and to sketch out plans for the classroom on graph paper, but since we're not in each room every day, how can we ensure that this culture continues to grow and flourish? Talking to principals about guaranteeing common preparation time and creating healthy and organized professional learning communities is often a good place to start. Volunteering to help out with almost anything teachers need is a good follow-up. Modeling what we hope to see and hear in each classroom is also valuable insurance. If the principal is on board with the idea of a renewed interest in the culture of literacy, we have a strong ally who has the attention of the faculty on a regular basis.

The bottom line, though, is what teachers see in their classrooms. If they create an enticing library and suddenly see a new burst of interest in books among their students, they are more likely to continue on the path to a culture of literacy. If they "bless books" by introducing one each day in a book talk and are then able to recognize that their students are "crazy" about reading those books, if they are flexible and decide to let some of their own books circulate, allowing children to take books home, if they encourage their students to write letters to each other by having mailboxes and mail deliveries in classrooms, and observe as their children become "rabid writers," they will have more than enough reason to maintain their efforts.

Teachers need a time and place to celebrate their successes. Perhaps at the beginning of each faculty meeting the principal could ask for each teacher to report a success, or one teacher could be recognized at each meeting for something small, but wonderful that happened as a result of his work. We need "success rituals"!

Celebrating Choice: The Joy of Book Clubs

Although many classrooms operate with all children reading one book in common, and others are organized around independent reading, book clubs are a wonderful way to introduce children to the joys of reading with a degree of choice in a social setting. Students respond well to the organic nature of the book club, and teachers often find that choice (of reading material or of partners) is a highly motivating factor. Reading is a social activity for many of us. When we read a book that inspires us or one that makes us laugh or cry, our first thought is to share that title with fellow readers—to let them in on the wonderful secret we have stumbled upon. When we gather to talk about a particular book and find our words being echoed by other readers, our joy is multiplied. It's natural to want to discuss a great book find with others, and book clubs allow children to share in this way. It is every teacher's wish to create lifelong readers; book clubs help us promote positive attitudes toward reading that will fuel that wish.

A marvelously educationally sound reason to teach using book clubs is that instructors are also able to teach skills and vocabulary in situ, rather than as stand-alone strategies and words. Seeing a word in print and figuring out its meaning from the surrounding sentences make the learning of vocabulary so much easier and more natural. No more lists of isolated words; on to understanding new language within the context of a story. Children see how the word is used by the author and are soon able to utilize the word in their own speech and writing. Words learned in this way stay in the memory longer.

The use of book clubs also relies heavily on student participation and responsibility. Discussions are student run, and it is rare to see a child who does not take part in her group's conversation. Anticipating that some pupils will be more willing to speak out than others, we can include mini-lessons that teach ways for children to reach out to encourage their more reticent friends to participate. This also shifts the responsibility for getting along and moving forward to the children themselves, taking some of the nagging out of teaching. Also, because books vary in page length, the group is held accountable for setting up and managing its time. Each group determines how much it needs to accomplish daily after having looked at the schedule provided by the teacher. Students learn a bit of time management here.

Book clubs are highly student centered. Since each child has a turn in making her own choice about which book she wants to read, every student has a voice, and that voice is respected. Increased choice often results in a stronger sense of responsibility. Children feel accountable, not only in their commitment to their work, but also to each other as group members. Engaging them creates a greater probability for cooperation and interaction within the classroom. Group work allows each pupil a voice

A table is organized with certificates and university gifts for students who have participated in an after-school reading club.

since even timid children feel safer taking risks in small groups. Our students may, therefore, hear more diverse responses, which can help them to look at the world from a different perspective. These student-led discussions evolve naturally and can lead to deeper and more critical thinking. Thought-provoking questions often lead to true reflection about how we responded to a theme or the craft of a particular author or to being questioned or challenged during group work.

Reading is a habit that we want to cultivate. It has been proven to increase our ability to focus and concentrate, improve our memory, reduce stress, and develop critical thinking, as well as serving as a lifelong source of entertainment. When integrated into a well-run literacy classroom, book clubs can intensify the joy of reading for teachers and for their students. (You will learn more about book clubs in Chapter 7.)

CONCLUSION

In this chapter, we shared authentic ways to refocus a joy for learning in school communities. In no way does our work suggest that everyone must be happy 100% of the time. We know that this is just not the case, and could be a somewhat superficial expectation. However, we believe that intentional engagement across the literacy community can reap great outcomes in myriad ways. Whether you are a classroom teacher, reading coach, reading specialist, or building administrator, you can take notice of students by building relationships. We can show students that we believe in their potential, while advocating for their rights to read.

Lit 💡 Idea

Find additional reading materials related to happiness and joy, and apply what you've learned to the classroom! When we originally got started with our work, we loved checking out resources like *Time* magazine's special edition *The Science of Happiness: New Discoveries for a More Joyful Life* (June 10, 2016). Get to searching for the latest materials and see where natural fits relate to your teaching or school/district environment.

Stop, Think, and Take Action

Based on the ideas presented in this chapter on engaging and joyful literacy leadership, take time to consider ways in which you might get everyone involved to support readers and writers in your local school community. Reflect on the following:

If your role is that of a . . .

- **Classroom teacher** or **teacher-leader**—Use Children's Rights to Read to set a personal professional development goal for the school year. Choose a right that resonates with your passion and belief that every child needs this right now.
- **Literacy specialist** or **literacy coach**—Consider where your teachers are in your school community. What are their strengths? What areas need improvement? Be sure to reflect

on who engaged readers and writers are in your school community, and who is often disengaged or unmotivated.

- **School administrator** or **school-level leader**—Build trust and prioritize goals. If a goal is important and needs to be a priority in your school, what can be taken off of teachers' plates so that more energy can be funneled into that need? Consider administering a brief climate survey with your staff: "What would make our school a more joyful community for readers and writers of all ages?"

- **District administrator** or **district-level leader**—Provide support for literacy initiatives that bring joy back into focus for readers and writers. The standardized test scores are likely to improve when district leaders, teachers, parents, and community members share in the literacy mission of the school community. Support your schools with ongoing financial support for books. What are some of the latest children's books, mentor texts, and novels that can breathe life into your district's curriculum? Seek out these resources.

- **Professional developer**—Find research related to workplace happiness. Infuse some of these elements into your PD icebreakers or into the overall design of your professional development. For example, you might decide to integrate ways to foster teacher capacity during your trainings (e.g., mindful moments, norms for staying in the moment).

CHAPTER 3

Telling Your School
or District's Literacy "Story"

Teachers are experts who know far more about the children
they interact with than do test makers. Teachers who are skillful
collectors and users of classroom-based evidence organize what
they know around principles of teaching and learning and the value
systems important in the communities in which their children grow.
—SUSAN MANDEL GLAZER

It's late summer, and the Hatchery Hill team meets to review standardized test reports.
Each person on the team has a different purpose for what will be gleaned from the data.
For certain, everyone agrees that the test is just a snapshot of what's happening in the
district. The team considers what story these data tell and what other forms of evidence and
explanations can be used to determine strengths and areas of needed improvement related to
the literacy program. Team members ponder over a few different kinds of questions.

MRS. GRIFFIN: Is there a trend across a grade level or grade levels? How does
performance compare with classroom observations (both formal and informal)?

MRS. CALABRESE: What trends exist across the schools I oversee? What unique needs
does each school have? Do the needs of a special population require a new and
innovative intervention?

MRS. ROSENFELD: How are various grade levels performing over time? Is there a grade
level or area that deserves special attention?

MRS. DEMARCO: Did my interventions work? What changes should I make to my
scheduling or use of instructional approaches? What structures are working or
need a second glance?

Later, the Assistant Superintendent, Mrs. Diskin, takes a panoramic look at the district
results and whether or not the literacy teams are making a difference in the lives of readers
and writers. She notes areas of success that deserve celebration and recognition, but also
finds funding to bring in a professional developer to target specific literacy needs. A date is

announced when Mrs. Schiano will get to meet with all of the teams to set a schedule for professional development aligned with the district and school goals for the school year.

WHAT WE KNOW ABOUT TELLING YOUR LITERACY "STORY"

In today's educational landscape, schools are able to use a variety of tools to self-reflect and paint a picture of the literacy "story" as it exists and is told. Standardized test reports provide snapshots of achieved levels of proficiency in reading and writing, resulting in additional reports that give leaders a sense of what standards were met and which ones remain to be achieved. Daily lesson planning and delivery of instruction shed light on curricular materials and best practices that are working and those that need additional fine-tuning. Ongoing intervention and referral services provide the literacy team with comprehensive solutions to addressing students' achievement and knowledge gaps. Parents, too, provide us with anecdotal evidence of whether or not the students are intrinsically motivated, independent readers beyond the confines of the school walls. Even school report cards published online provide rankings of how our schools are performing when compared to other schools, and anyone who has purchased or tried to sell a home within the last few years will know that the achievement of the local school is often tied to the perceived value of homes and to higher rents. So with the stakes being the way they are, we advocate for digesting what's at our fingertips and finding personal joy in seeing hard work pay off.

EVALUATING YOUR CURRENT PROGRAM WITH AN HONEST EYE

In Chapter 3 of *Breaking Through the Language Arts Block: Organizing and Managing the Exemplary Literacy Day* (Morrow et al., 2018), a plethora of tools that teachers can use to assess for both students' literacy achievement and instructional planning is introduced. Although this type of assessment drills down to making informed decisions about what students need for whole-group, small-group, and one-on-one assistance, there are also broader ways in which assessments can be used to honestly answer the bigger question: Is our approach to literacy instruction meeting the needs of our learners? In this book, we seek to highlight how confident teachers and administrators feel about the approaches that increase the joy in teaching and learning. As opposed to a deficit model (e.g., "We aren't doing well on behalf of our English learners"), we seek an approach in which data spark new *curiosities, interventions, and innovations* (c.g., "We have the tools and the staff to create and design a Bienvenidos Book Club"; see Chapter 9). In order to collectively excite teachers and literacy leaders regarding such approaches, a number of practical assessment strategies are discussed in this chapter.

Assessing the Literacy Landscape

We refer to the term "literacy landscape" to broadly describe what it looks like, feels like, and sounds like when literacy leaders commit to working together in positive

A data wall is designed to celebrate students for top literacy growth and performance.

ways to impact readers and writers across grade levels. Ideally, this landscape is evident as soon as you walk into a school building. The environment is warm and welcoming, and both teachers and students are happy to be a part of their learning community. There is evidence in hallway and classroom displays that the school makes literacy a priority. In this literacy landscape, the administration advocates for a time when teachers, reading specialists, and coaches can meet to prioritize and monitor goals, effectively analyze data, and plan quality instruction. Literacy truly becomes a community priority, with families attending literacy events that may occur during or after school (see Chapter 9).

Importantly, the conversations are focused and enthusiastic. Teachers and students work together to discuss texts, and students can often be found deep in conversation, dissecting aspects of a text or even peer editing their writing with the support of others. In essence, our readers and writers enjoy being in school.

Listening to Teachers' Stories

Classroom teachers are constantly orchestrating various materials, programs, and approaches to deliver high-quality instruction daily. Therefore, we show great respect for teachers when we seek their input as to what seems to be working and what would make coming to work even better. The five-question survey in Figure 3.1 is one way to gather valuable feedback that helps teachers thrive at this worthwhile work.

Teachers: Help Us Improve Our Literacy Landscape

1. Consider the comprehensive literacy program that our school/district offers at your grade level. What do you consider to be our strengths? What areas would you suggest need improvement?

2. Do you feel that you have been well trained to orchestrate the literacy program? If not, what professional learning opportunities are you interested in?

3. What materials, if any, are on your "wish-list" for enhancing student learning (e.g., latest children's books, mentor texts)?

4. What suggestions do you have for increasing engagement among faculty, staff, parents, and other members of our literacy community?

5. Is there something non-literacy related that would make coming to work more joyful (e.g., parking spots, water coolers)?

FIGURE 3.1. A sample five-question survey for classroom teachers regarding the literacy landscape.

Lit 💡 Idea

Literacy leaders can meet as a team to develop a calendar of "surprise and delight" moments that can take place throughout each month. Perhaps you would like to surprise a teacher with a book based on personal interests, or maybe you would like to decorate a teacher's parking space with the cover of his or her favorite novel. The opportunities abound!

Listening to Parents' Stories

Parents, too, deserve a voice in the implementation of the literacy landscape. Their stake in how their child's school operates and in the culture that the school exudes is huge. If we hope to call upon them for assistance during the school year, their thoughts should also be solicited and respected, for example, by using the short survey in Figure 3.2. (Further discussion of engaging parents takes place in Chapter 9.)

Interpreting Data for Use in the Classroom

When teachers think about what it is that brings joy into their classrooms, it's likely that data are not exactly near the top of the list. However, when data are used appropriately, the information can be incredibly helpful in ensuring that the teaching and learning occurring on a daily basis is necessary, important, and meaningful. There are many different types of data that teachers and administrators can utilize to drive instruction, and in this section we'll be looking at which data may be the most useful, how to analyze data effectively, and how to use data to design instruction that is exciting, engaging, and joyful. Yes, you read that correctly. We're going to spark joy through the use of data!

There are a variety of formal reading assessments that can be used to determine students' reading levels, as evidenced by the fluency and comprehension strengths

---

Parents: Help Us Improve Our Literacy Landscape

1. Do you feel that you are kept informed about the literacy work being taught and accomplished in your child's classroom? If not, what might help?

2. Does the teacher "know" your child as a literacy student? Is he or she aware of your child's strengths and challenges? What else does he or she need to know about your child?

3. Is there a topic or area in literacy you'd like to help deliver to our students? What hours are most convenient for you?

4. What school events do you participate in? What others would you like to see offered?

5. What literacy story (or reading/writing experience) from your family can you share?

FIGURE 3.2. A sample five-question survey for parents regarding the literacy landscape.

and areas in need of improvement for each individual student. They may include the Developmental Reading Assessment (DRA2), Fountas & Pinnell Assessment Benchmark Systems, Qualitative Reading Inventory–6 (QRI-6), Gray Oral Reading Test—Fourth Edition (GORT-4), and others. Although the reading level itself does give the teacher some information about a child's instructional needs, it is important to get a broader perspective in order to truly inspire reading growth in each child. For example, we certainly do not want to label students by their levels and teach all "M" readers the same way. Even though the level will provide insight as to which skills and strategies students should be capable of utilizing independently, there will be strengths and areas of need that vary from child to child. As such, formal reading assessments provide a solid starting point, but should be considered as a piece of the reading puzzle, not the finished product.

Did you know that the anecdotal notes you take during your reading groups, strategy groups, and one-on-one conferences are excellent sources of data? Looking at the quantitative data gleaned from the assessments we've mentioned, which give us the numbers to chart growth, is important. However, the qualitative data that you collect on your students will enable you to really learn about them. Looking back at the comments that students made while conferring helps you to understand the thinking and learning that is taking place. Tracking these data points over time will show growth. Many teachers overlook this source of data, thinking that it doesn't qualify, because they assume data have to be quantitative and based on numbers. Not true! When you bring qualitative data to the table for consideration alongside the quantitative, you can now have a comprehensive view of who the child is as a reader. Don't underestimate the importance of the observations you make about your students while you listen to them read, observe them write, or discuss their work and thinking with them.

One of the most incredible aspects of data collection is the limitless number of opportunities it provides you as the teacher. Is data analysis always fun? Of course not. However, what it will show you is exactly where you need to go for each child. Consider it a road map to success. Reviewing benchmark data or other quantitative data and finding a gap in a student's understanding shouldn't be disappointing—it should be exciting! You now have a starting place where you can effect *real change* and *real learning* for this student based on his specific and unique needs. Not only are you able to identify an area in need of growth and plan all of the exciting ways you can approach intervention instruction, you now have a baseline from which you can track the student's growth. That, truly, is the exciting part. When you reassess a student and determine that he has shown growth, even the smallest bit, in the area on which you were working, you have the opportunity to celebrate it. And celebrate it, you should! Any small success students achieve should be celebrated. It helps build their self-esteem and self-confidence, and it allows them to see themselves as successful readers. Perhaps this small success leads to a student taking bigger risks or pushing a little further the next time he's reading a text, and that is just what we're always looking for from our students as they grow.

Still, there is an area with untapped potential on which we haven't yet touched. Sure, it's exciting when we find that a student has demonstrated growth, and we get to celebrate that child's hard work. But what if the student noticed his own growth? What if he walked, or ran, to your desk with a huge smile because he realized he's achieved what he's been working toward? It does not get much better than that. So, how do we get there? We're so glad you asked! Self-monitoring of goals is a task that can be accomplished by students from the lowest grade levels up through college and beyond—as long as it is modeled and presented appropriately. The goals can emerge from anywhere. Perhaps you review benchmark or assessment data with a student (yes, even a kindergartener) and, together, look for an area in need of improvement. Perhaps you ask the student what he, himself, thinks he should be working on—an area in which he doesn't feel quite as strong or a skill he doesn't feel he's quite mastered. These are goals in which students themselves now have a vested interest. They've helped determine them. They have ownership of the process. You, as the educator working with this student, will guide him, of course. Some students will need more assistance than others in selecting a goal that is reasonable, personal, actionable, and important. You will help them to determine the next steps: What can they do to achieve their goal? How will they know that they have achieved it? You will confer with them and always at least touch on that goal to check in and show that you are also interested in and excited about their growth toward their goal. Your job is to keep the train on the track, always moving in the right direction. Will there be roadblocks and wrong turns? Of course there will! But, you will be there to help students regain traction, and you will be their biggest cheerleader when they realize that they have achieved their goals, which is what the joy of growth in reading is all about.

Effective Data Analysis

Recently we visited a school where the collaborative team placed a picture of the child at the center of the table whenever discussing his or her literacy needs, keeping foremost in our minds that these children are at the center of our work, and a holistic approach is often employed. Beyond taking into account the child's reading level, we must look into how well we can answer the following questions:

- How does the child identify as a reader/writer?
- Does the child articulate specific goals related to reading and writing?
- How much independent reading and writing occur both in and outside of school?
- How is the child developing his or her phonological awareness, phonemic awareness, phonics, fluency, vocabulary, reading comprehension, and writing?
- What motivates and engages the child?
- What is the child's reading or writing attitude?
- What has been done in the past to remediate any concerns? What approaches were successful, and with whom?
- What other information is helpful to know?

Using these questions and a variety of literacy assessments and tools as a guide, literacy changemakers can effectively speak to the strengths and needs of each individual child. In other words, we are using data to understand the whole child and not just one prioritized piece that stands alone.

Using Data to Drive Instruction

In the following chart, we highlight some beliefs that are important in utilizing some of the most common forms of support for readers and writers.

Literacy practice	Belief
Strategy groups, guided reading, small-group differentiated reading, book clubs, inquiry circles, etc.	This group has the potential to articulate what strategies are working and why they help them as readers. They are equipped to monitor their own understanding of the text and go deeper with comprehension even on their own. They have a set of goals with outlined steps on how to get there.
Reteaching	One size does not fit all when it comes to mastering skills in reading and writing. There are always other approaches that might be a better fit for the students I'm working with.
Intervention	Tiered systems of support are important for meeting the needs of learners, but the stronger my Tier 1 instruction, the better off my students will be. I can look into what works for individual learners and connect with literacy experts to best teach and reach each learner.

What about Exceptional Learners?

Although many schools will provide support for helping children (especially those who are striving) reach levels of proficiency in reading and writing, it is also important to engage literacy leaders in a discussion of how the needs of exceptional learners are being met. It is broadly recognized that these learners have exceptional needs, talents, learning styles, and behaviors that fall outside of the "norm." For example, we must take a look at how the literacy needs of students with disabilities are met, while also advocating for the students with gifts and talents. In Figure 3.3, we share some of the available resources, with a commentary about how these resources can be used to contribute to your school or district's literacy story. It is our belief that literacy changemakers are inclusive and resourceful leaders who avail themselves of multiple ways of understanding and of seeing beyond "boxes" or departments within a school or community. Whether it's curriculum and instruction, ESL, special services, or other areas, we are here on behalf of the literacy needs of all learners and must work together to be part of the integrated support system that our kids so deserve.

English Language Arts Program Evaluation Options

Once data are collected and analyzed by individuals and teams, there is an option for literacy changemakers to evaluate the bigger picture and determine the next steps

Resource	Literacy look-fors
Smith, C. B. (1991). Literature for gifted and talented. *The Reading Teacher, 44*(8), 608–609.	• Does the literature selected address both the cognitive and affective needs of gifted learners? • Are the scope and sequence of the program based on the latest research and theory related to meeting the needs of gifted learners?
Carris, J. (2011). Reconceptualization: Inclusive and empowering literacy education for non-reading adolescents. *Counterpoints, 361,* 113–133.	• In what ways are we currently making literacy fun and engaging for struggling (striving) readers? • How are we designing instruction around our learners, rather than forcing our learners to adapt to our instructional design?
Lemons, C. J., Allor, J. H., Al Otaiba, S., & LeJeune, L. M. (2016). 10 research-based tips for enhancing literacy instruction for students with intellectual disability. *Teaching Exceptional Children, 49*(1), 18–30.	• What are the "big-picture" literacy goals of the school/district? • Is this vision articulated with respect to including students with intellectual disabilities? • What explicit and systematic reading instruction is utilized? • What data have been analyzed to guide instruction and adaptation?
Stanberry, K., & Swanson, L. (2009). Effective reading interventions for kids with learning disabilities. Retrieved from *www.readingrockets.org/article/cffcctive reading-interventions-kids-learning-disabilities.*	• A strong instructional core • Focus on increasing students' word recognition skills • Differentiated strategies for increasing students' reading comprehension • Tailored adaptations to curricular programs and materials
Self-esteem resource: *www.readingrockets.org/helping/self-esteem.*	• How do our teachers respond to discouraged readers and writers? • How do our students feel about themselves? • In what ways can we help foster a sense of confidence by providing truthful, ongoing words of encouragement toward all students?

FIGURE 3.3. Resources for supporting exceptional learners.

for continuous improvement. In Figure 3.4 (at the end of this chapter), we take you through one way of gathering as much detailed information as possible. While this can be a lengthy process (anywhere from 6 to 18 months in most schools), the information gathered and reported on is invaluable and can be adapted based on consensus.

Lit 💡 Idea

Agree on which literacy changemakers will do what and according to what time line. For example, you may want to assign roles (or have roles for leaders to choose from) based upon individuals' expertise. Roles can include, but are not limited to, literacy historians, best-practice finders, data diggers, parent/community liaisons, literacy interviewers, and instructional observers. While it may also serve in the team's interest to learn what's working in nearby school communities, embrace your own district's mission, values, and strategic plan first. Ensure that any perceived role models, are, in fact, aligned with your beliefs. Do your work at home first.

CONCLUSION

Your school community's literacy "story" should not be a fictitious tale about which students are passing or failing in general, but rather should be a collective effort to assess the comprehensive needs of readers and writers and determine how the programs and practices should be carried out. It's an opportunity for literacy changemakers to rumble with what's actually taking place to support readers and writers and to find innovative ways to answer lingering questions or find solutions to perceived problems. It is our experience that these curiosities lead to new interventions and programs specifically aimed at helping our students excel.

Stop, Think, and Take Action

Based on the ideas presented in this chapter on telling your school or district's literacy story, take time to consider the ways in which you might take part in the research, on-site visits, or reporting of the assessment data gathered by the group of literacy changemakers in your school or district. Reflect on the following:

If your role is that of a . . .

- **Classroom teacher** or **teacher-leader**—Take a look at your anecdotal notes and class roster. Identify two to three students who would benefit from a classroom-based literacy evaluation and intervention. Reach out to the literacy specialist to collaborate. Consider choosing students who need that extra push to gain confidence or self-esteem.
- **Literacy specialist** or **literacy coach**—Once challenges across a grade level, school, or the district have been identified, research strategies that might be helpful for teachers and students. Model lessons, meet with PLCs, and conduct book clubs that deal with these areas to increase awareness and fill the gaps.

- **School administrator** or **school-level leader**—Communicate with your team about the importance of classroom visits, and reiterate that these opportunities provide teachers with time to "listen and learn," and not evaluate. Be willing to collaborate or even co-teach with a teacher who appears hesitant about the process.

- **District administrator** or **district-level leader**—Gain support from your local board of education members or curriculum committee about the importance of conducting a thorough English language arts program evaluation if one has not been conducted in the past in your school district. If one has been conducted, review the results and revisit the chapter to determine if any missing pieces would paint a broader picture.

- **Professional developer**—It is important to begin with the strengths of the district and to give credit to initiatives that have a track record for (1) being aligned with effective literacy instruction and (2) initiating student growth. At the same time, be honest about what's not working and offer solutions for where addressing the problems can begin.

Step 1: Convene a team of literacy changemakers and find out what information is already available. How many students are advanced proficient, proficient, approaching proficiency, or not yet proficient? Seek information from any and all grade levels (typically 3–12).

District Name _____   Date(s) _____

ELA School Profile

School Name _____

ELA Achievement Results	Year 1					Year 2					Year 3				
ELA Levels of Performance	L1	L2	L3	L4	L5	L1	L2	L3	L4	L5	L1	L2	L3	L4	L5
	% of students					% of students					% of students				
Grade 3															
Grade 4															
Grade 5															
Grade 6															
Grade 7															
Grade 8															
Grade 9															
Grade 10															
Grade 11															
Grade 12															

Notes about data trends (utilize various reports):

Grade	Trends
K	
1	
2	
3	

(continued)

FIGURE 3.4. District-level K–12 literacy program evaluation.

Grade	Trends
4	
5	
6	
7	
8	
9	
10	
11	
12	

Step 2: Get out in the field and take a look at what's going on. You may want to include a literacy professional developer to facilitate this experience. Some guiding questions that we have used in school districts to support teams are listed below. What stands out?

Guiding Questions:

1. Does the school have a literacy teacher leadership-team structure? Y N
2. Is there a reading specialist? Y N
3. Does the school have a systematic plan for reading intervention? Y N

(continued)

FIGURE 3.4. *(continued)*

4. What materials are used for literacy instruction? _____

5. How is the curriculum adopted? _____

6. Do benchmarks and pacing guides exist?   Y   N

7. What assessments are used? _____

8. Are teachers participating in PLCs, grade-level meetings, and other forums?   Y   N

9. Is there vertical articulation?   Y   N

10. What type of past professional development has occurred? _____

11. Are teachers thoroughly trained in implementing the standards?   Y   N

12. How is professional development selected and funded? _____

13. Describe the overall school culture/environment. _____

14. Are there before- and after-school programs?   Y   N

15. Does the school receive Title 1 funding?   Y   N

16. What is the school's philosophy about literacy instruction? _____

17. What is the school's collective definition of rigor? _____

18. Is literacy integrated into specials (art, music, etc.)?   av   Y   N

General Notes:

Observations:

1. Is the room neat and organized for whole-class and small-group instruction?

2. Is the environment literacy rich?

(continued)

FIGURE 3.4.   *(continued)*

3. What activities occur (how long and when)?

4. How are the following components being taught?
   - Phonemic awareness

   - Phonics

   - Vocabulary

   - Comprehension

   - Fluency

   - Writing

5. How is literacy instruction organized?

6. What happens during guided reading?

7. How are students assigned to independent/partner practice (i.e., work stations)?

8. What do students do during independent/partner practice? Are they on task?

9. How is differentiation handled?

10. Is reading integrated in the content areas? How? What interdisciplinary approaches are used?

11. Do students engage in project-based learning?

12. What roles do the different adults in the room play?

Notes about general classroom culture (i.e., interactions, language, respect/rapport, atmosphere, etc.):

(continued)

FIGURE 3.4. *(continued)*

Step 3: Organize your findings! What are the best activities for readers and writers that are taking place currently? What are the areas in need of improvement?

Step 4: Now it's time to prepare a formal report and possibly a formal presentation for local literacy stakeholders. What next steps will bring your school community forward? What will bring more joy to literacy learning in the classroom? Start with the positive!

FIGURE 3.4. *(continued)*

CHAPTER 4

Rethinking Professional Development and Professional Learning Communities
Teacher-Centered Opportunities for Authentic Buy-In

If you want to go fast, go alone. If you want to go far, go together.

—AFRICAN PROVERB

Like many schools across the country, Hatchery Hill is not immune to the trepidations surrounding professional development and improving practice. The chart in Figure 4.1 highlights some of the common ailments and symptoms of school communities that have these worries and the growth mindset that's needed to develop better instruction for our kids. Check out the chart and see where you fit now or where you've "been."

KNOWLEDGEABLE LITERACY PARTNERS: WE CAN AND MUST DO BETTER FOR OUR KIDS

While it may seem a bit ironic to begin a chapter in a book on bringing the joy back into focus as literacy changemakers with a list of roadblocks, we understand the sometimes harsh realities that can often get in the way of finding better solutions for learning. Perhaps we have even found ourselves brought into the world of the "naysayers," and felt comfortable in being a part of their community. Even if at times we felt "off," we were picked up and dusted off with a good old-fashioned reality check from one of the more joyful literacy changemakers in our lives. Whatever the reason may be, it is important to recognize the roadblocks, identify the negativity in our spaces for what it is, and choose a better way.

Inspirational speaker Baruti Kafele (@PrincipalKafele) reminds us that in addition to an achievement or attitude gap, there is also a gap between educators who have the will to be amazing at their craft and those who do not. In choosing to read

The "naysayers"		Our literacy changemakers	
Teacher	"This too shall pass. Next year they'll be onto the next initiative, and won't even notice I haven't made any changes in my classroom."	Mrs. DeMarco	"I may be a seasoned teacher, but I'm open to learning new ideas and practices and seeing where they fit in based on my students' needs. Let's do this!"
Reading specialist/ coach	"It feels like every year a new program or practice is added and nothing is ever taken away."	Mrs. Rosenfeld	"Let's look at this new research and see where it fits in with our strengths and where we might need to improve or take away some things."
Supervisor	"These teachers can't be trusted. I wonder if this new initiative is computerized and tracks compliance."	Mrs. Calabrese	"It's been awhile since we've provided PD around this area of need. Let's get our team together and get this done!"
Principal	"Our building doesn't need support. The schedule is a disaster, and contractually I don't see how this is going to get done."	Mrs. Griffin	"We always learn so much when we bring in new ideas. Let me look at the building schedule and support a time and place for our initial PD. We can look at options for making this work."
Assistant superintendent	"How much money is this going to cost the district? We invested in literacy initiatives last year and barely saw an increase in our test scores."	Mrs. Diskin	"I know this is going to take a 3- to 5-year commitment. I'm willing to stick this out if we empower the team and align our next steps with our district strategic plan."
Professional developer	"This school feels hopeless. From the moment I sign into the main office I feel the roadblocks and even resentment at times. They certainly are in need of my support."	Mrs. Schiano	"We've seen incremental changes that are worth celebrating. In just a few short months, more people are getting on board. We can carry out this initiative and make a difference!"

FIGURE 4.1. Potential roadblocks versus growth mindset solutions.

this book, we know where you stand and welcome you with arms wide open. In this chapter, let's work together to learn how to turn around any negative feelings you may be observing or harboring when the acronyms PD, PLC, or PLN (OMG!) leave the lips of your literacy peers, and instead get passionate about what professional growth and development hold for our presence as literacy leaders.

Creating an Enjoyable and Relaxed Atmosphere for Learning

When we talk about professional development, there are two types of teachers, and you definitely know them both: Type A *loves* PD and can't wait to learn and try new things. Type B would rather be anywhere *but* PD and may be skeptical and/or disengaged before even walking through the door. A popular meme on social media pokes fun at this phenomenon; in it the latter teacher believes that dying during PD wouldn't be so bad, as the "transition from life to death would be so subtle." The million-dollar question is this: How do we celebrate and create early adopters from Type A while also getting through to Type B?

The providers of PD are often administrators, and they may have unknowingly fallen victim to something that leads to an absence of several crucial aspects defining meaningful, successful, and effective PD. There is a terrible syndrome out there, and we like to call it "administrator amnesia." It is so vitally important that, no matter how many years you have been out of the classroom, you always remember what it's like to be "in the trenches." This advice applies to every aspect of leadership, but certainly to planning PD.

Think about the conferences, seminars, and workshops you attend. Think about the way their design makes you feel:

- What makes you energized?
- What makes you wish you could sneak out through the back door?
- What engages you and makes you excited to learn more about how you can improve your own practice or bring strategies back to your classroom, school, or district?

The PD you plan needs to achieve all of these aims, and a smart place to start is the atmosphere you create from the very moment your teachers walk through the door. PD should be *filled* with joy, as it is where teachers will grow, share, and find ways to improve their own practices as well as influence change in the practices of their colleagues.

One of the things the authors collectively love to do is set the stage for PD with a jovial, high-spirited, and energetic approach to teachers' first impressions of the session. This may include playing lively, fun background music or including treats like the "chocolate salad" referenced in Chapter 1. While these enticements seem like

FIGURE 4.2. A sample introductory slide at a PD event using Bitmojis from *www.bitmoji. com.*

an inconsequential aspect of your setup, walking into PD can elicit different waves of feelings over teachers, from anxiety to excitement to hesitation. Teachers are left alone with their thoughts in a silent room, and we want those thoughts to stay positive! Additionally, we have been known to include silly Bitmojis on our title slide (see Figure 4.2) to keep the introductory remarks and expectations light and playful (while also keeping us on track with what to share and when). A presenter's overly serious or earnest tone at the outset of PD can denote a session without joy and, for those reading between the lines, that can mean no personality and no fun! While the topics we discuss in our PDs are always important and intended to drive change, it is powerful and engaging when the presenter's authentic positivity, personality, and passion are woven into every aspect of the session.

Lit 💡 Idea

If you find yourself in charge of planning PD, begin with some type of "surprise and delight" moment. Perhaps it's asking the audience about their favorite Beatles song or offering a few book giveaways to help teachers assemble more robust classroom libraries. This positivity will not go unappreciated or unnoticed by participants. If you are a participant, pay attention to your presence. What does your presence say at the PD?

DRIVING CHANGE THROUGH FLEXIBILITY, PERSONALIZATION, AND PRACTICALITY

There are few things worse in PD than being disappointed by sessions or workshops that you were looking forward to. Have you ever been excited about PD until you realized it

- wasn't applicable to you in your position or with your population?
- didn't take into account your prior or background knowledge?
- was laser focused on something that wouldn't translate to your practice?

When presenting PD, keep in mind that the teachers who attend may possess a vast array of experiences, levels of expertise, needs, and expectations. How can you make sure that the PD you provide is not only a good use of their time, but also leads to a change in mindset or practice? Sometimes we have the ability to "take the temperature" of the staff prior to PD through surveys or conversations. Even when working in the environment in which the PD is occurring, it is important to ensure that you and the attending staff members are on the same page. Ensuring that the teachers' needs are what you perceive them to be will allow for more productive PD that moves everyone in the right direction.

Needs assessments can be sent to the staff prior to developing your PD session. The administration may have a goal in mind in terms of what your focus should be, but it is still crucial to ask the staff what their current needs are surrounding that intended focus. Teachers need not only to *feel* heard but actually *be* heard, as demonstrated through the PD that is delivered. Collaboratively developing professional learning that takes into account the needs of the teachers alongside the needs of the administration will lead to outcomes in which both parties feel that important work has been done and experience a shared sense of accomplishment and a mutual understanding of the next steps.

Lit 💡 Idea

Read Katie Cunningham's (2019) book *Start with Joy* to find amazing resources and activities designed to promote student happiness. Of course, many of the activities work very well with teachers and school communities, too!

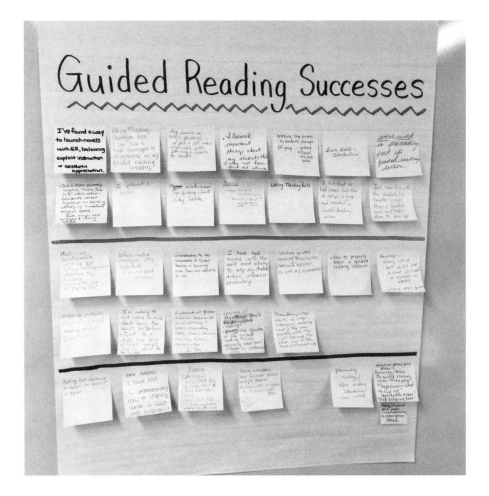

An anchor chart displaying teachers' recent successes with guided reading instruction.

However, sometimes it isn't possible to administer needs assessments ahead of time. That doesn't mean that PD shouldn't be personalized to meet teachers' needs and their current level of understanding. This is the point at which initial activities and conversations with attendees are vital. You may decide to ask teachers to fill in an "entrance slip" on which they will jot their experiences, beliefs, prior knowledge and understandings, and questions. In reviewing or discussing this information, you may find that the teachers already possess a wealth of knowledge on the PD topic, leading to a decision on your part to increase collaboration and sharing of professional experiences or successes that may be useful to colleagues. You may decide that it's necessary to shift your focus from one section of your presentation to another, or you may skip over certain topics entirely. This shouldn't be cause for alarm or panic. You now have a beautiful opportunity to capitalize on what you know about your attendees and what *they* know about the topic!

Giving teachers an "entrance slip" upon arrival can also allow you to frame the PD or continue to set the tone for the session. The example in Figure 4.3 shows how you can immediately focus teachers' attention on your topic and motivate them to engage actively.

Two key takeaways to consider as you design your PD are practicality and applicability. If what you teach and discuss today can be implemented tomorrow, there is a much greater potential that teachers will not only engage more actively during the session, but will also put what they learned into practice, which can involve stepping out of their comfort zones. This means delivering a session filled with ideas that are relevant and that you can authentically stand behind as a leader. This also means avoiding PD that overwhelms teachers with too many ideas and strategies. The best PD is often a deep dive into one or two strategies. After these sessions, teachers will feel more confident in their ability to implement the strategies, because there has been a significant amount of time spent ensuring understanding and planning for next steps.

Lit 💡 Idea

Some of our favorite PD or professional learning opportunities seem to have a "Monday Morning" takeaway. In essence, there is something new and exciting from the learning opportunity that doesn't require hours of planning, a second master's degree, or an entire prep period to prepare for. It's a freebie that teachers can use right away (e.g., a graphic organizer based on the latest comprehension research, a helpful website or person to follow on Twitter, a new book that you *must have* for your classroom library, or a lesson plan that's already written for you). You get the idea. Something is provided that can be implemented in your classroom seamlessly on a Monday morning.

It will be your job to help teachers understand not only how to incorporate new learning into instruction, but also why it is important and beneficial for them and for their students. Put yourself into the teachers' shoes and consider how you could

> 1. Jot down some notes about what makes reading joyful for you. What gets you excited about reading?
> 2. Complete the following sentence: "Reading makes you feel good because. . . ."
> 3. When is reading great?
> 4. When is reading not so great?
> 5. What have you been reading lately?

FIGURE 4.3. A sample "entrance slip" to be used at the start of PD.

realistically include the ideas discussed in PD in lessons that teachers have already planned. One of the easiest ways to encourage teachers to take immediate action is to ask them to plan an upcoming lesson during your session. This approach also allows you to support and guide them, celebrate their willingness to take risks, and plan follow-up activities. These follow-ups can be as simple as a quick email to check in or popping into a teacher's classroom to see how the lessons went. Not only does this demonstrate to the staff that the work is important, but it also shows that you care and have a genuine interest in helping them feel successful in their practice.

Speaking of demonstrating that the work is important, let it be stated loud and clear: very rarely does anyone benefit from "fly-by" professional development. If you've been an educator for any length of time, you know exactly what this is: a 1-day, one-shot PD that no one ever talks about again. What typically results from PD like this? Quite literally, nothing. No shift. No change. Sure, teachers may give the ideas a try, but PD will not be sustained. Essentially, it is the opposite of the goal of successful professional learning. When we as leaders do not continue the discussion and check in with teachers on the implementation of concepts and practices from our PD, we send a message that it is not worthwhile and that we will not be supporting them in improving their practice. Every PD session should be planned with specific and scheduled follow-up activities. They could involve a second session, a discussion in which successes and challenges are shared, or one of the scariest, but most important and exciting practices we can put into place: scheduling teachers to informally observe (or to listen and learn from) one another in the classroom.

This practice, often referred to as "fishbowling," can be frightening for teachers at first. It takes courage to invite colleagues into your classroom to observe a lesson! However, there is so much to be gained from this activity. Not only can the observed teacher receive feedback on what the observers noticed, what went well, and where there is room for growth, observers will also walk away with opportunities for self-reflection and ideas for ways they can improve their own practice. It should be noted that these observations are entirely informal. They should not be used by administrators as walkthroughs, observations, or any other aspect of the evaluative process. Teachers who invite others into their classrooms are taking a risk and will likely feel a bit vulnerable, especially when this practice is first attempted. At the onset of this professional practice, it will take a few brave souls, who may need some coaxing, to volunteer as observees. However, this is important and exciting work. Why is it so important? This is PD that is as authentic as it gets. It does not involve an administrator, coach, or other PD provider telling teachers what they should do. Rather, it is learning from colleagues teachers know and trust and to whom they have ready access for questions and advice. The practice won't translate to your staff as a wildly successful idea overnight. In time, however, you will find that teachers offer their classrooms not only to demonstrate best practices, but also to ask colleagues for support and feedback in areas where they may feel something is missing from their own teaching. When you have a staff willing to take those risks, you have something very special that needs to be encouraged and supported by the school and/or district leadership.

Administration backing is imperative for this practice to be successful. The teachers will need logistical support to ensure that classes are covered and that appropriate coverage by a substitute teacher is secured for the observation period. It is also advisable to set aside time that is designated solely for debriefing. Fishbowl observations have little power if there is no follow-up discussion. What you will often discover in these conversations is a rich dialogue, in which participants cite specific examples of what they saw that impressed them, what they want to know more about, or what they are excited to try themselves. You will also find constructive feedback that makes the process reciprocal. When implemented appropriately and carefully, everyone wins! In addition to logistical support, teachers will need moral support when preparing for fishbowling or debriefing. It can't be overstated—this is often a scary prospect in the beginning. Your job as a leader is one of reassurance. Everyone has something to gain from the process, and it can help establish a professional community of collaborators where both doors and minds are open for change and growth.

Lit 💡 Idea

If you are reading this book because you are excited about literacy and want to establish yourself as a literacy leader, this is a great place for you to start. Take the first step by asking your administrators to help you set up fishbowl sessions in your classroom, either to share a part of your practice about which you are confident and excited or, if you are feeling very brave, to solicit feedback in an area you would like to improve. Sometimes all it takes to start the domino effect is one teacher initiating the process, and what a great step in your leadership journey to be that teacher!

At the opposite end of the spectrum, if you are reading this book because you are already a literacy leader, you now have a fantastic opportunity to begin strengthening your internal capacity for leadership. Think about the teachers, specialists, and coaches you know who are truly outstanding in different areas of their practice. Reach out to them and tell them you think they rock! (See Figure 4.4.) Ask for permission to invite teachers into their classrooms to learn from them. Of course, getting an invitation may take some coaxing, but when we build up teachers' confidence by providing genuinely positive feedback, they will be more willing to open up their classrooms to their colleagues. When a school reaches this level of collaboration and collegiality, it can be sensed from the moment you walk through the doors. There is great joy in

FIGURE 4.4. A sample invitation to host a "listen and learn" literacy session. Drawing by Isabel Casais.

learning communities that celebrate teachers as the experts they are and recognize them as providers of PD through the sharing of their practices. In these environments, teachers understand, and truly believe, that they are wholly valued for their expertise, creativity, leadership, and experience.

OPPORTUNITIES FOR HANDS-ON DESIGN

As an administrator or teacher-leader, think about the best lessons you have seen or have taught. What makes them great? Is it the lecture? The knowledge imparted to students by the teacher? Not likely! What makes a great lesson is often the dialogue, the thoughtful contributions of students, the collaboration among students (especially when the teacher can step back into the role of facilitator), and the independent or collaborative work that is developed as a result of the lesson. When designing PD for educators, we should be following our own advice! If we tell teachers not to solely lecture to their students, we should not be lecturing to our teachers during PD. Where does that leave us? In the best place possible—a PD environment that takes into account the needs of our adult learners and gives voice to the attendees.

One of the greatest benefits for teachers in PD, as we discussed previously in this chapter, is the ability to take whatever has been learned and either replicate it or incorporate it immediately. However, this doesn't just happen on its own, and it certainly doesn't happen effectively if the teachers have sat through a PD session only listening without *doing*. Would we ever expect a student to demonstrate proficiency in a reading strategy without modeling it before providing an opportunity for guided practice? Of course not. This is true of our adult learners, as well. Sometimes we are sharing professional development about fun and exciting ideas that teachers can use in the classroom. Fun and exciting doesn't mean that the ideas won't be intimidating to try on their own. While we all know teachers who will jump right in with two feet and give anything new a try, others will need to wade gently into new activities. Giving teachers the opportunity for hands-on work in our sessions provides that gentle wading time that many of them need. This allows teachers to go through the trial-and-error aspect of new learning under your supervision and with your assistance and, most important your encouragement! Not only will this boost teachers' confidence, but they also will have the chance to ask questions, determine how to effectively incorporate new learning into upcoming lessons, collaborate on-topic with colleagues, and be more likely to make sustained use of the learning in their practice. The added bonus? They'll have more fun! Any time we can break away from the lecture format in our PD and focus the learning on teachers' practice, where it should be, we are on the right track.

Lit 💡 Idea

Have you ever heard the observation "A noisy classroom is a happy classroom"? We love walking into classes to see and hear students happily working and discussing ideas. An energized class is a great indicator that students are taking charge of their learning and are putting new learning to use. The same should be true of PD. Always look for ways that you can get teachers working collaboratively, and not solely relying on turn-and-talks! Consider your PD topic. Have teachers participate in an actual activity, so they understand what it should look like in their classrooms. Then ask them to do the real, important work of planning how to incorporate what you've taught them into their upcoming lessons.

DESIGNING THE "DREAM" PROFESSIONAL DEVELOPMENT PLAN: A CALL TO ACTION

Whether you are a teacher-leader or school or district administrator, you know that remaining silent when PD is being planned can have adverse effects on what's to follow, including, but not limited to (1) PD that is not aligned with the school or district's goals and strategic plan, (2) PD that is irrelevant to what the teachers need or want, and (3) PD that does not intentionally address the needs of the students. The template in Figure 4.5 is a guide for planning for "dream" PD. When completing the template, consider the tips and subjects that were discussed earlier in the chapter, and

Professional Development Proposal for _____ (school name)

Year: _____

Literacy Changemakers:

_____   _____

_____   _____

_____   _____

Professional Development: (Briefly "sell" why this PD is important and needed.)

Example: _Last year, our students achieved greater heights when it came to comprehending fiction and informational texts. The literacy team believes that the strategies brought back to the district after attending the Rutgers Reading Conference made all the difference. The proposal below is respectfully submitted by our literacy team. The team will complete appropriate district paperwork for all events that are approved._

Event	Date	Cost	Rationale

What's Hot at _____ **School**

According to our faculty/administrator surveys, the following literacy topics are "hot" or deemed really important at the moment:

-
-
-

Significance: The latest "What's Hot" report from the International Literacy Association (2020) (_www.literacyworldwide.org_) addresses these areas that are directly aligned with what we would like to learn more about in order to better our practice:

-
-

FIGURE 4.5. A planning template for "dream" PD.

collaborate with literacy changemakers or "thought partners" who are just as excited about literacy learning as you are. Then collaborate and get to work on something amazing—something BIG!

Professional Learning Communities for Literacy

As the authors of this book, we assert that there is joy in knowing that all professional learning communities (PLCs) support the literacy development of students. We have seen school communities where PLCs are formed in a variety of ways and structures. Some are based on grade levels, while others are based on departmental needs (e.g., ELA, science, math). Some schools form vertical teams or "houses" where students are supported throughout the network of grades, as teachers collectively advocate for a common set of students. Many PLCs also band and disband depending on factors related to personal interest or advancing the strategic plan of the district or building-based goals for improvement. If the disparity in structure and arrangement alone is not enough to confuse the reader, add to the mix questions related to what happens during PLCs and how often they actually meet. Although one can vaguely categorize a PLC as any group with a vested interested in education, DuFour, DuFour, Eaker, Many, and Mattos (2016) suggest that we ask ourselves: (1) Are students learning, and how do we know?, (2) What does the culture of collaboration look?, and (3) What are the results?

With these considerations in mind, the PD team can support PLCs by reading their professional development proposals, suggesting events, and determining which offerings will meet the needs of the most teachers, giving the district the biggest bang for its buck.

Lit 💡 Idea

Determine whether or not the PD in your school aligns with the Children's Rights to Excellent Literacy Instruction (Dwyer, Kern, & Williams, 2019). Will children have more knowledgeable and qualified literacy educators as a result of the PD? Will the support systems be more integrated? Will the PD result in more supportive learning environments or greater numbers of high-quality resources? Will the PD address equity?

CONCLUSION

In this chapter we discussed the ins and outs of quality PD. We advised that districts listen to the perceived needs of their teachers through the work of PLCs. We discussed the value of choosing PD that is a "just right fit" for the teachers who will be taking part in it. We also gave advice to those who conduct PD, hoping that they would inject joy, or even a bit of fun, into their presentations. As with students, an interactive presentation goes a long way toward making sure that the material worked on in PD will be carried into daily practice to the benefit of children.

Stop, Think, and Take Action

Based on the ideas presented in this chapter on rethinking PD, take time to consider the ways in which you might create more teacher-centered opportunities around literacy learning. Reflect on the following:

If your role is that of a . . .

- **Classroom teacher** or **teacher-leader**—Participate in surveys to ensure that your voice is heard. Consider the comprehensive literacy needs of your students (e.g., phonemic awareness, phonics, fluency, vocabulary, reading comprehension, writing, motivation, and engagement). Advocate for professional learning that will help you move your students forward and create better equipped super readers and writers.

- **Literacy specialist** or **literacy coach**—Look back at the chapter and list two or three actions that you will plan as a result of the information learned. What is next on your list to accomplish? What ingredients will you include to make the professional learning or PD more enjoyable for teachers?

- **School administrator** or **school-level leader**—Think outside of the box when choosing an area of professional learning that would benefit your teachers, and, therefore, the readers and writers in your school community. Perhaps a "Fluency Friday" or a "Word Nerd Wednesday" will showcase best practices. "Motivation Monday" could feature book talks as part of the morning announcements. The opportunities are endless, we know—so just get started with one of them or choose your own adventure!

- **District administrator** or **district-level leader**—Be sure to set aside appropriate funding for professional learning opportunities. If funding is limited, what innovative opportunities exist for your teachers to increase their literacy repertoires (e.g., live-streamed events, online training/classes)?

- **Professional developer**—So much of this chapter could be considered devoted to you or to the PD team collectively. Now, do something! As we like to say, it's time to read, research, and reach out to experts. As the head cheerleader for current literacy best practices, these three R's are extremely valuable.

CHAPTER 5

Recalibrating Literacy Programs
What Makes the Best Learning Environment?

Students want to be understood and should be expected to share their voice as part of the learning process. The school and classroom should be safe places where students can express their honest opinions and concerns, ask questions, and have meaningful decision-making opportunities. When students believe they have a voice in school, they are seven times more likely to be academically motivated!

—Doug Fisher and Nancy Frey

Mrs. Griffin realizes that transforming literacy environments is not a "1-year thing." Although Mrs. Rosenfeld assessed that the classroom libraries were in need of more informational texts last year, she has recently heard from teachers like Mrs. DeMarco, who now would like to bring in more diverse and inclusive book collections. Mrs. Calabrese has advocated for a healthy resources line in her budget to acquire more books yearly. Mrs. Diskin has approved this budget, witnessing during school visits and classroom evaluations the joy that new titles have brought to the classroom teachers, the students, and their families. At a recent visit to Hatchery Hill, Mrs. Schiano introduced the leadership team to the International Literacy Association's "Teachers' Choices" lists of favorite mentor texts. The teachers have begun to peruse the book lists to choose some exciting new titles to include in the classroom libraries, and many have recommendations of their own.

RECOGNIZING WHAT MAKES FOR THE BEST LEARNING ENVIRONMENTS

When it comes to fostering a learning environment where students are motivated, engaged, and empowered to realize their potential as readers and writers, a focus on the design of the classroom is crucial. Through collaboration with peers like Debbie Diller (2008) and our work featured in Chapter 2 of *Breaking Through the Language Arts Block: Organizing and Managing the Exemplary Literacy Day* (Morrow et al., 2018),

A welcoming school stairwell includes uplifting messages for students.

we continue to assert that our spaces and places mean the world to the students who occupy them daily. We start with culture, or the literacy lifestyle of the classroom, and move into the climate, or mood, that permeates it throughout the day. We then discuss the physical environment (e.g., books, print, space, and time). Joy is at the heart of each of these key elements as we consider, not necessarily achieving the "best" space for learning, but most definitely, striving to be better than we were yesterday.

CULTURE AND CLIMATE

Along with the planning of the physical environment at the beginning of each school year, we recognize a cultural element that must be present to build a joyful classroom. Fisher, Frey, Quaglia, Smith, and Lande (2018), refer to this element when they speak of the "invitational stance to learning" (p. 6). In their book they cite Purkey and Novak (1996), who discuss invitational education as having four important elements. The first is trust, indicating the idea that both teachers and students demonstrate confidence. Both groups believe that the other's intent is positive and have the desire to create relationships.

The next ingredient in an invitational classroom is respect. This is, of course, built upon the knowledge that everyone has value in the shared community created in a classroom. We see this in a room where put-downs are not tolerated and where diversity is welcomed.

Optimism is the third component in the invitational classroom. While it is clearly an expectation that the teacher keep things positive and believe in the potential of each student, we emphasize that students are also expected to support their peers as all of them learn and apply a plethora of literacy skills and strategies. Joyful classrooms are hopeful and optimistic places!

The fourth element is intentionality. Nothing comes without effort, and although this effort may be joyful, it is always intentional. It requires that everything that happens in the classroom (or in the school community) has been designed to "convey trust, respect, and optimism to all" (Purkey & Novak, 1996, quoted in Fisher et al., 2018, p. 7).

Teachers who invite students to learn have a huge effect on the learning that takes place. It is very telling that only 55.7% of students who responded to a survey (Quaglia Institute, 2019) said that they believed that teachers made an effort to get to know them. This effort begins with the necessity of learning what students wish to be called. Names hold a student's identity, and pronouncing and knowing them is an important start. Remembering names becomes harder once teachers have multiple classes, but it remains vital. Children's names, of course, are not all that we need

A teacher creates her own "READ" poster to self-identify as a reader.

to know about them. A teacher who is invested in her students and in their success knows what is important to them, be it their favorite music, or what sports or pastimes they are passionate about. It does not take much time or effort to get to know children. They want to love us, and they deserve a teacher who cares about them. For the same reason, we should allow our kids to get to know us a little. We're not sharing everything, but we can let them know that we used to ride horses, that we love to hike, or that reading is our favorite pastime. This sharing of knowledge and understanding can go a long way and enhance the culture (lifestyle) of the classroom.

If it is our desire to create a joyful classroom, we must begin with healthy student–teacher relationships. We have said earlier in this book that teachers who love coming to work cultivate students who love coming to school, and that kids who enjoy being in school achieve more than their unhappy counterparts. If our children do not believe that we know and care about them, building a relationship will be a very difficult task. Healthy and happy teacher–student relationships are built on trust, respect, honesty, and communication. We cannot assume that our students know that we care about them. We need to communicate that to them daily through demonstrations of honesty and respect.

In a local school in New Jersey, the literacy coach and the school's technology specialist joined forces to showcase the reading lives of all of the school's personnel. They asked teachers, custodians, classroom aides, the school principal, and lunch workers to pose for their cameras reading a book. They blew up and laminated the photos and posted them outside the spot where the school workers spent most of their time. Students pause outside of classrooms, the gym, and the cafeteria to notice that the adults in their school have reading lives, and perhaps they begin to decide that they should, too!

"Hatching" Each Child

Indulge us for a minute as we weave an analogy. One of us (and only one of us) raised chickens for several years. Since the school on which our work in this book is based is named Hatchery Hill, let's talk about how teachers "hatch" and grow learners using a chicken-raising analogy. The chicken raiser among us advises that you must enter the coop daily with a feeling of pure joy about raising your chickens. On some days you pick up the latch, and the birds peck at you. On other days you enter a truly stinky space, one that you must keep clean and dry. Once in a while the hens are "broody and moody," and don't want much to do with you. You, however, love raising your chickens, and you carry that joy with you as you continue to talk to them, to feed them, and to round them up to go back into the coop so they are protected from predators each night. When it's cold outside, you buy your chickens a small heater for the coop and warm their mash before you feed them. It doesn't matter what you are met with in the coop; you remain calm and joyful. You demonstrate your joy and love for the chickens no matter what. If you think of your classroom as your coop, you will see that doing your work well actually feeds your joy—as a teacher or a chicken farmer!

If you're still with us on this journey through the literacy environment, consider these fun connections:

- *Culture*—Raising chickens is no doubt a unique lifestyle, and so is teaching! When your relatives and friends refer to your teaching method as "Aw, that's so cute," you must refocus the attention on the urgency, joy, and relevance for why hatching readers is important for the world in which we live. Literacy is a mission.
- *Climate*—The mood of the coop can change on a daily basis, but some common elements remain. If the chickens have confidence in knowing that they will be protected and fed, the rest comes quite easily (with some days that are harder than others). Our students need to know that their classroom will be a safe and protected learning environment where readers and writers can take risks in order to thrive.

Now, let's dig into the features of this coop (er, we mean classroom).

Access to Books

Some of the recent research related to access to books demonstrates that there are actual "book deserts" in our communities, where students have few, if any, books at home, in addition to limited access to books outside the home. Organizations such as BookSmiles and Little Free Library are working diligently to promote neighborhood book exchanges in the form of "public bookcases" and public opportunities for teachers to get free books into the hands of their students.

Teachers undoubtedly need to have access to high-quality classroom libraries. When designing a high-quality classroom library that is both interdisciplinary and inclusive, some general recommendations can be applied (Booksource, 2019; Lee & Low Books, 2017; Morrow et al., 2018; Routman, 2003; Scholastic, 2019b). Using some of the latest checklists and tools for designing such spaces, researchers Drs. Ken Kunz, Jason Fitzgerald, and Michelle Schpakow from the Monmouth University School of Education in West Long Branch, New Jersey, recently created the checklist in Figure 5.1, synthesizing some of the most commonly used classroom library

A Little Free Library in New Jersey (*@farview-littlefreelibrary* on Instagram).

Statement	Yes	No	Weed it or need it?
General Recommendations			
Books are organized with a balance of genres, levels, authors, featured books, etc.			
There are approximately 15–30 books per student (or 300–750 books overall) (7 books per student for a novice teacher).			
Two books per child are added to the classroom library annually.			
Leveled texts, decodable readers, and complex texts are available if needed.			
Diverse formats include, but are not limited to books, magazines, catalogs, diaries, ebooks, and audio books.			
Materials for reader response include Post-it Notes, writing paper, graphic organizers, colored pencils, etc.			
There is a 50/50 balance of fiction and informational texts.			
Books are in good condition.			
Genres include, but are not limited to picture books, chapter books, poetry, folktales, joke/riddle books, historical fiction, mystery, science fiction, fantasy, biography, classics, series, multicultural, nonfiction, graphic novels, etc.			
Author study collections and series collections are included.			
Contemporary choices/high-interest books are included.			
Award winners and book list choices are included (e.g., Newbery Award, Caldecott Award, ILA Children's Choice, and Teachers' Choice).			
Reference materials are included (e.g., thesaurus, dictionary, atlas, picture dictionary).			
Clear labels and signage are included within the classroom library.			
Books are easily accessible for all learners.			
Book displays include books with covers facing outward to entice readers.			
Literacy displays and props are located in the library area.			
A management system for recommending books to peers is utilized.			
A management system for checking out books is utilized.			
Students are able to make book recommendations (e.g., use of interest inventories).			
The classroom library is a welcoming focal point of the classroom.			
The reading area includes flexible seating (e.g., rugs, beanbags, pillows, chairs).			
The reading area includes soft lighting and decorative items (e.g., plants) to create a warm and homelike feeling.			

(continued)

FIGURE 5.1. A sample interdisciplinary and inclusive classroom library checklist. Created by Kunz, Fitzgerald, and Schpakow (2019); based on Booksource (2019); Lee and Low Books (2017); Morrow, Kunz, and Hall (2018); Routman (2003); and Scholastic (2019).

Statement	Yes	No	Weed it or need it?
Time is allocated for students to "shop" for books, and students are not limited by reading level.			
Independent reading time is part of the daily class schedule.			
Interdisciplinary Topics			
Books represent various geographic locations worldwide (e.g., Asia, Africa, Europe, Central/South America, Oceania, Indigenous Regions, North America).			
Geographic locations represented include rural, urban, and suburban settings.			
History/social studies topics are included.			
International studies are included.			
Peace and postconflict topics are included.			
Science, Technology, Engineering, Arts, and Math (STEAM) topics are included.			
Environmental topics are included.			
Business and economic topics are included.			
Religious topics and religious holidays are included.			
Health and wellness topics are included.			
Books addressing mindfulness are included.			
Inclusivity			
Books feature cultural and linguistic diversity.			
Books include main characters who cope with challenges or loss.			
Books include main characters of color.			
Books include main characters who are LGBTQIA+.			
Books include main characters with disabilities.			
Books feature contemporary diverse characters and story lines.			
Books feature a range of family structures and family configurations.			
Books feature characters with different types of gender identity/gender expression.			
The classroom library features diversity throughout the year.			
A diverse cast of characters or inclusive images are represented in nonfiction.			
Diverse protagonists are included (e.g., African American, International, Latino/a, LGBTQIA+, Middle Eastern, Indigenous).			
A variety of authors and illustrators are represented (e.g., African American, Asian, Jewish, Latino/a, Muslim, Indigenous, LGBTQIA+).			
A variety of cultures are represented (e.g., African American, Asian, Jewish, Latino, Muslim, Indigenous, LGBTQIA+).			
A variety of perspectives and experiences are included (e.g., financial hardships, immigrant experience, indigenous people, LGBTQIA+ themes and studies, people with special needs, people with physical disabilities, refugee experience, women's history).			
The classroom library is reflective of the students in the class (e.g., gender, race, family diversity, language, culture, socioeconomic background) and/or provides a window into the diverse lives of others.			

FIGURE 5.1. *(continued)*

checklists. In their work with a local school district, the team is exploring to what extent the current setup of classroom libraries in a local grades 3–5 elementary school is meeting the needs of students and teachers. When using the checklist, it is important to first determine whether or not the general recommendations and the interdisciplinary and inclusive components are present in your classroom library. If so, decide whether the collection needs to be weeded, or thinned out, owing to aging materials, overabundance, or even a lack of student interest, or whether some books are deemed unnecessary for other reasons. You must also determine the gaps, and identify areas that need additional books.

Lit 💡 Idea

Instead of "Who wants to read this?," Scholastic Library Ambassador John Schumacher encourages teachers and literacy changemakers to instead ask, "Whose heart needs this book?" For additional ideas about book talks, refer to Chapter 7.

An active lending library has an open-faced display for students to borrow books.

A well-stocked library allows teachers to borrow books according to author and genre, while accessing materials for intervention.

A high-interest, low-readability library has been organized according to increasing text complexity by genre to help teachers borrow materials as they help readers progress.

Print: Begin with Your Word Wall

In an elementary classroom the word walls (alphabetized and holding frequently used words) are placed at a level where children can see them and are able to interact with the words daily. Children look at these word walls to find how to spell their most commonly used words, and the words therein eventually become "no excuse words," because no one has an excuse for ever misspelling them. The words are generally taken from the Fry or Dolch word lists (Morrow et al., 2018), and children may play games with them during work station time. Once children learn to recognize and use these words, their joy in reading increases, since primary books utilize these words with great frequency, and children feel empowered as readers when they can read them. In upper-elementary classrooms, the words on the wall may vary, because the teacher recognizes the words that her students commonly misspell or misuse and places them on this word wall.

Lit 💡 Idea

Chant it out! In high-energy classrooms, we will often observe the teacher (or one or two students) lead the class in sight-word chants. Some suggestions for having fun with the students are included below. Just make sure that the students are paying attention to the individual letters and words in addition to the fun and interactive movements.

Format:
_____ the letters, and _____ the word!

Some possibilities:
The Swimmer (*swim, dive*)
The Chop and Sweeper (*chop, sweep*)
The Movie Star (*brush hair, flip a mirror*)
The Basketball Star (*dribble, shoot*)
The Hockey Player (*skate, shoot*)
The Volcano (*raise, explode*)

. . . or create your own with the students!

Vocabulary Word Walls

Most classrooms also have a space for new vocabulary words to be displayed. Effective teaching includes increasing word consciousness: raising the awareness of readers and writers for new and beautiful vocabulary. These words, sometimes called "power words," "juicy words," "spicy words," or "college words," are placed on display for as long as possible after they have been introduced and explicitly taught so that students are able to use them in their written work. There's nothing like seeing the joy on the face of a child who has just been commended for using a power word in a composition! For a longer discussion of word walls and vocabulary word walls you can check out our last book (Morrow et al., 2018) or read about some of our latest favorites in the Lit Idea shared here.

Lit 💡 Idea

Get your hands on these amazing professional resources. These texts help us realize our potential in making vocabulary learning fun and interactive.

- *Word Nerds: Teaching All Students to Learn and Love Vocabulary* (Overturf, Montgomery, & Smith, 2013)
- *Vocabularians: Integrated Word Study in the Middle Grades* (Overturf, Montgomery, & Smith, 2015)
- *Bringing Words to Life, Second Edition: Robust Vocabulary Instruction* (Beck, McKeown, & Kucan, 2013)

Anchor Charts

Well-designed anchor charts support learning in dynamic and memorable ways (see Figure 5.2). The best charts are created with our students, and remind them of strategies they have been taught, but that may not have solidified in their minds yet. If we ask, "Why charts?," Roz Linder (2014) reminds us that anchor charts have many benefits.

- Children have a shared sense of ownership over their content. Charts belong to the whole class.
- Kids will use them! These charts have an impact on instruction.
- Visuals are engaging! Having engaging visual reminders of lessons teachers have taught triggers the memories of our students and keeps their attention.

ANCHOR CHART High Five

- Alignment with standards and best practices
- Authentic
- Age-appropriate language
  - Academic language
  - Words students know, use, and can read
- Attractive and memorable
- Accessible and visible to students

FIGURE 5.2. The "Anchor Chart High Five" demonstrates five components to keep in mind when developing and using anchor charts with students.

It's important to recognize that not all the anchor charts that we create must remain hanging in our classrooms for the entire school year. There is such a thing as too many charts. A few important ritual and strategy charts are eye catching; 50 of them are an eyesore. Over the years we have seen some terrific ideas for repurposing charts. First, when they have outlived their use, hang them on skirt hangers. At the end of the year dole them out to eager students who will use or play with them at home. Take pictures of the charts and glue them into students' reading or writing notebooks. Keep a copy of the photos of all of your charts, so that you'll be able to recall them for next year when you create them again with a different group of kids.

Lit 💡 Idea

If you are unable to part with your works of art, hide your beautiful anchor charts in the closet until you are ready to share them with the students. The following explanation can be used when revealing the new chart. "I recently took our ideas from the sloppy-copy chart that we created, and added some ideas of my own in addition to yours. Check it out!"

Space

By now you are probably imagining an environment that feels cozy and homelike—a classroom where you could spend the entire day (or even a snowstorm). All kidding aside, we experienced a snowstorm a few years ago during which students ended up sleeping overnight at one of our colleague's schools. Pictured in the photograph, who wouldn't want to spend the night in Dr. Carmen Gordillo's classroom? In this

A middle school classroom library corner in West Orange, New Jersey.

classroom, we can see that a small-group meeting area has been designed to meet the diverse needs of students who will want to kick back, relax, and collaborate over books. Our classrooms need whole-class, small-group, and one-to-one areas for conferring about reading and writing. Most important, these spaces need to be well organized, appealing, and uncluttered.

Lit 💡 Idea

Toss, restore, and organize within your classroom. Disorder in environments can be a drain on the positive energy and happiness that we seek. If one study can cite the effects of decluttering on reducing housework in the average home by 40%, imagine what decluttering could mean for the classroom learning environment. Take time to declutter and get your room in order, even if it involves the students contributing their own ideas and solutions (Rubin, 2015).

Time

"When will I find the time to do this?" It's a common question that we are often asked by our colleagues in the field. Time is, as we find ourselves repeating so frequently, the enemy! Teaching lives are often a battle between what is important and what we have time for. In *Breaking Through the Language Arts Block: Organizing and Managing the Exemplary Literacy Day* (Morrow et al., 2018), we even feel somewhat guilty at times when we admit that "exemplary" is what we strive for. In a world where every day holds unexpected outcomes, the sun rises and gives us this awesome opportunity to meet the needs of learners who enter our learning spaces. And while some days may knock us down a notch or two, who wakes up to be mediocre? Instead, we need to stretch our time and our reach. This begins with having a learning environment that is welcoming and structured, limiting potential distractions or interruptions. It includes teachers who see the value in integrating literacy across content areas, and we're not just talking the language arts folks, either! In one school we visited, the physical education teachers had a bulletin board featuring vocabulary related to sportsmanship. Students were encouraged to take copies of *Sports Illustrated Kids* articles related to athletes who rise above the rest. An urgency for learning is present, and time for reading and writing is protected across the school day and in various contexts. Let's continue to strive for what's exemplary.

CONCLUSION

Humans respond to their surroundings. They don't always recognize that they are doing so, but they do. If their world is neat and orderly, they generally feel better than if they live in chaotic surroundings. If they have access to the tools needed to learn, learning is easier and comes more naturally. When the people around them recognize their worth, they feel valued and better able to work toward a goal. So too it is with children. When they believe that their teachers know and care about them, when they feel safe and respected, they work hard and achieve. Of course, it's not as simple as that, but joyful and caring classrooms produce caring and happy children.

Stop, Think, and Take Action

Based on the ideas presented in this chapter on what makes the best learning environment, take time to consider the ways in which you might enhance the environment in your own "coop." Reflect on the following:

If your role is that of a . . .

- **Classroom teacher** or **teacher-leader**—Look for surveys you can administer to all of your children in September. There are surveys that ask about children's learning styles, about what's important to them, about their likes and dislikes, and how motivated they are about reading. Administer these surveys and, even better, spend some time talking with each child individually about his or her answers. Learn the names of each child in your classes.

- **Literacy specialist** or **literacy coach**—Call attention to new surveys (or create them with PLCs specifically for their children) that allow kids to "have a voice" in their classroom. Model lessons in classrooms that demonstrate how to use the survey results to motivate individuals or groups of kids. Get to know as many names of students as possible. It matters.

- **School administrator** or **school-level leader**—You, too, should try to learn students' names. If certain children are sent for discipline regularly, consider talking, working, or reading with them instead of or in conjunction with behavior modification.

- **District administrator** or **district-level leader**—Create a fun internal competition with awards for different literacy learning environment categories (e.g., best reading nook, best display of student work, most cozy one-to-one conference area, most inviting student recommendation area).

- **Professional developer**—Meet with PLCs to discuss the findings of John Hattie, the man upon whom Fisher and Frey's work is based. It will amaze the PLCs to learn how easy it is to bring joy back into the classroom beginning with trust, communication, and honesty.

CHAPTER 6

Recalibrating Literacy Programs
What Works for Early Literacy?

By learning from the most exemplary teachers—teachers who "beat the odds"
in helping all their children achieve thoughtful literacy—we can create
classrooms that work even better than they have in the past.
　　　　—PATRICIA M. CUNNINGHAM AND RICHARD L. ALLINGTON

While every teacher at Hatchery Hill has a unique set of strengths related to the effective
teaching of reading and writing, the leadership team is committed to a comprehensive
approach to literacy instruction. Mrs. Griffin believes that solid Tier 1 instruction in the
classroom will lead to higher levels of student achievement. Mrs. Calabrese and Mrs.
Rosenfeld agree and have continued to ensure that joy is at the center of all professional
development and learning. Ongoing professional development that addresses phonemic
awareness, phonics, fluency, vocabulary, comprehension, writing, and *student motivation
and engagement* has been provided. This focus is aligned with the district strategic plan
reviewed by Mrs. Diskin, who agrees that comprehensive literacy instruction includes social
and emotional learning. The team meets with teachers like Mrs. DeMarco and asks, "What's
working with our early learners? What lights up our students' eyes with excitement? What
needs a second glance?"

FOUNDATIONS FOR EARLY LITERACY INSTRUCTION

Keeping in mind that our book focuses on the aspects of joy that are tied to literacy
instruction, we celebrate writing during a time where our own state is recognized as a
national leader for student achievement and as having the number-one public schools
in the country (Loyd & Harwin, 2019). Of course, we also recognize that our top
performance still leaves room for growth. Like many high achievers, we value striving for an A over having achieved the B+. Our state spends a significant amount of
money on education in general, but early literacy has been a particular focus. What's
more, joyful learning communities have something very significant in common: they

don't just dream or philosophize about comprehensive and balanced literacy instruction; they make the vision of an exemplary day part of the everyday school culture and climate for our earliest learners (a structure explained earlier in Chapter 1). These schools bring the components of comprehensive literacy instruction to life (National Reading Panel Report, 2000), weaving in high levels of student motivation and engagement, home–school partnerships, and robust intervention programs delivered by skillful teachers who love what they do. These schools have classrooms that work, in which children are actively reading and writing throughout the day and instruction is, quite honestly, just plain fun. Reading coaches and school administrators can connect with the feeling you get when you could imagine staying in that energetic early literacy classroom all day long, but also know the feeling you get when spending 20 minutes in another one feels like an endless forever. Join us on a joyful literacy journey of the energetic classroom.

Choosing Happiness: A 10-Month Calendar

In Laura Nielson's children's book *Mrs. Muddle's Holidays* (2008), readers are introduced to a quirky neighbor on the block who chooses to celebrate the oddest of holidays, taking time to appreciate nature and the little things around us that we sometimes take for granted. The students are confused by her actions at first, that is, until they begin to find joy in silly celebrations like "Let's Pretend It's Summer Day" in the middle of winter or "Earthworm Appreciation Day" at the first signs of spring. What if we intentionally brought this same level of excitement to our early literacy classrooms? With topics like mindfulness gaining momentum, one can understand the importance of taking the time to intentionally be present and joyful in the classroom. Books like Katie Cunningham's *Start with Joy: Designing Literacy Learning for Student Happiness* (2019) provide some engaging activities for refocusing that energy with kids specifically, noting that, of course, students want to be stronger readers and writers, but they also hope to be happy in our classrooms. So, why not create a 10-month calendar that will keep them excited and engaged all year? After all, being happy increases our energy as literacy changemakers, and increased energy makes it easier for kids and adults to engage in activities (Rubin, 2015). Inspired by Stahl, Flanigan, and McKenna's (2020) Tell Me What You Like! survey, we offer the interest inventory in Figure 6.1 as a way to get started in getting to know your students at the beginning of the school year.

After administering the interest inventory with your class, it takes just a little bit of time and energy to notice trends. These trends can become special celebrations each month, as students will look forward to a school year calendar focused on the things that bring joy and happiness to their lives. Selfishly, the classroom teacher should also choose a celebration based on his or her own personal or family interests. Use the template in Figure 6.2 to engage in your own version of a happiness project (Rubin, 2015), and set aside time during each month to feature and showcase these topics through some celebrated theme-based lessons that can include, but are not limited to (1) engaging and intentional read-alouds; (2) vocabulary meetings; (3) phonological awareness, phonemic awareness, and phonics games; and (4) independent/partner reading. These affective factors play an important role in the literacy development of young

What Brings You Joy?

Name _____

Only put a check mark ✓ next to the statement if it brings you joy and happiness.

_____ attending or watching a sporting event	_____ singing my favorite songs
_____ playing sports	_____ cleaning my room
_____ getting a book as a present	_____ getting a high-five from a friend
_____ helping someone in need	_____ listening to a bedtime story
_____ playing video games	_____ visiting new places
_____ watching television	_____ playing board games
_____ playing with animals	_____ spending time outside
_____ finding insects	_____ staring at the sky
_____ spending time with my friends	_____ dressing up as pretend characters
_____ dancing to music	_____ hearing or telling jokes
_____ watching a magic show	_____ helping someone cook in the kitchen
_____ solving mysteries	_____ getting a hug from someone special
_____ swimming in a pool or ocean	_____ playing on a computer or device
_____ eating my favorite food	_____ reading a favorite book
_____ writing a letter or story	_____ counting or solving math problems
_____ solving a problem	_____ celebrating holidays

What else makes you happy? Write, draw, and label in the space below:

FIGURE 6.1. An interest inventory for learning what brings the students joy.

Teacher's Name _____ Class/Grade _____

10-Month Happiness Calendar

Month	Topic	Special Dates	Materials Needed
September			
October			
November			
December			
January			
February			
March			
April			
May			
June			

FIGURE 6.2. A planning form for celebrating 10 months of joyful learning.

learners and cannot be underestimated with regard to the planning that teachers are often in control of. Morrow (2020) states, "The teacher needs to be a decision maker who thinks critically about the design of his or her literacy program and the selection of materials. Children come to school with diverse social, emotional, physical, and intellectual abilities and achievement levels. They have diverse cultural backgrounds, experiences, and exposures to literacy" (p. xxi). Why not decide to choose happiness as a launch to the literacy learning that will occur throughout the school year?

> ## Lit 💡 Idea
>
> If you find yourself unsure of how or where to get started, launch the school year with a celebration of students' names. Throughout the month, designate special days to recognize the talents and interests of the students in your class. Provide a small brown lunch bag for students to create an "all about me" bag with small artifacts and a family photo.

Using Your Reading Foundational Standards

Once you cultivate a positive relationship with your students and get to know who they are and what brings them joy and happiness, you probably also recognize that you play a crucial role in their early literacy development and are aware of a startling, yet important, fact commonly cited in literacy research communities: Students who are not reading on grade level by the end of third grade are statistically likely to never catch up. Let's turn this outcome around with a comprehensive approach designed to meet students' individual needs. We have foundational standards for reading that tell us *what* to teach, and through engaging and interactive activities, we can address the *how*. The first step is to become familiar with the standards and use them as you plan your exemplary day (Morrow et al., 2018). Let's begin with phonological awareness.

Phonological Awareness

We know that teachers in early childhood settings play a significant role in helping students develop their oral language. They create opportunities for children to rhyme, to play with sounds and alliteration, to count the number of words in sentences, and to clap the syllables in words (Cunningham, 2017; Ehri, 2004; O'Connor, 2011). In Figure 6.3, we list simple and more complex tasks associated with phonological awareness, and identify some fun ways to center these tasks in the literacy classroom.

Phonemic Awareness

As students develop phonological awareness, they begin to get ready for phonemic awareness and progress to a more advanced (and more complex) level. They begin to recognize individual phonemes and can start to manipulate those sounds in words (see Figure 6.4). For additional word study techniques, we encourage you to read *Word Study That Sticks: Best Practices K–6* (Koutrakos, 2019).

Learning task	What it looks like in the early literacy classroom
Word Counting: Surprise Sentences	As students enter the classroom, they are greeted by a surprise sentence placed on their desks or posted in the whole-class area.
	The daily affirmation reads: There is no one better to be than myself.
	The teacher invites students to read the sentence with their partners. This is followed by echo reading, choral reading, and word counting with a pointer.
Catch a Name Beat and Check-In	Students gather on the carpet for a vocabulary meeting. As they prepare to choral-read the message, the teacher passes around a small rhythmic instrument (e.g., tambourine, maracas, drum). Students take turns rhythmically sharing the syllables in their names: "Hi, everyone. I'm Ra-chel (*drums beat*), and I'm feeling great today! I'm checking in for vocabulary meeting!"
Rhyme in Line	As students prepare to line up for recess or lunch, the teacher calls students by their onsets and rimes:
	"Start with an *M* (*mm*), add an *-aureen,* put them together, and we have . . ." Students shout: "Maureen!"
	Depending on the time available, the teacher may pick only a few names from a cup each day to showcase students throughout the week. Students excitedly listen for the sounds.

FIGURE 6.3. Interactive games that develop students' phonological awareness.

Learning task	What it looks like in the early literacy classroom		
Hold It, Say It, Sort It (adapted from Koutrakos, 2019)	*Example:* It's October, and you have decided that since your class overwhelmingly loves insects, you will allow them to vote for their favorite. The morning polling results are in, and it looks like ladybugs, it is!		
	You invite students to the whole-class meeting area on a Fun Friday to allow students to practice listening for sounds and comparing the sounds in words.		
	In a mystery bag of insects, you have cutouts of bugs that begin with the sounds /l/, /s/, and /c/. You sound stretch the /l/ in ladybug to model the activity, and place the ladybug in the /l/ column.		
	The mystery bag is passed around for students to pull out insects: ladybug, locust, lacewing, stick insect, stinkbug, cockroach, and cricket.		
	The pictures are sorted under the appropriate columns drawn on the whiteboard.		
	Noticing that students are so engaged in sound stretching and learning the names of both familiar and unfamiliar insects, you find an ABC guide for insects online to plan for another day in the month to celebrate through phonemic awareness.		
	l	s	c

FIGURE 6.4. A sample interactive game for developing students' phonemic awareness.

Phonics

Blevins (2019) reminds us that learning basic phonics skills will lead the reader to greater success with fluency, therefore opening up a world of possibilities for a child to comprehend and write. The question isn't whether or not phonics is an integral part of early literacy instruction, but what that instruction should look like in the classroom. Many of us remember the days of countless worksheet and workbook pages out of context, or, even worse, assigned homework to practice words three times each with no value or meaning. If anything, these types of tasks may have resulted in arguments at the dinner table or efforts to complete the tasks that led astray from the intended purposes. For example, studying the digraphs /ph/ and /th/ is useless if a homework assignment encourages students to write the words over and over again. The learner falls victim to strategies we have all used, such as creating columns to write individual letters in a row, as we fail to care (or recognize) the unique /ph/ or /th/ digraph. We still cringe when we walk into classrooms where students are encouraged to "rainbow write the words." And while some in the field of literacy pitter back and forth over what they believe is most important, we have to cut through the rhetoric, be clear and honest about our evidence, and find ways to do better on behalf of our kids (Pearson, 2019). When students need support with phonics, we know the characteristics of effective instruction we can draw from. However, we also advocate for comprehensively understanding the needs of the students who are trusted to our care daily. If 90% of a kindergarten class has phonemic awareness and recognizes the letters and sounds of the alphabet, one can question whether a phonics-heavy approach is the way to go? Likely not.

For students who need additional support with phonics, Figure 6.5 provides some opportunities for reinforcing explicit and systematic approaches that can engage the entire class.

Lit Idea

Ditch those weekly spelling tests! Instead, conduct diagnostic assessments to analyze the repertoire of spelling knowledge. Adoniou (2019) offers the following chart to guide analysis.

Think about it: would you rather have deep analysis of two to three words per week for students or an assessment of spelling words from a list that students have seemingly committed to short-term memory?

Actual word	Student spelling	Phonology (Is the spelling phonetically plausible?)	Morphology (number of morphemes spelled correctly)	Orthography (Does the spelling demonstrate knowledge about letter pattern conventions?)	Etymology (Is there any etymological knowledge that would help spell this word?)
coach	coch	Y	1/1 (co)	Y Student may need assistance with long-vowel patterns (/oa/)	*coche*: Middle French
Total		1/1	1/1	1/1	

Resource: To determine the etymology of a word, check out *www.etymonline.com*.

Rather than correct the spelling mistakes of our developing readers, we must celebrate their linguistic development. Instead of giving feedback about which spellings are right or wrong, ask yourself:

- Can you identify strengths?
- What are the areas of weakness or in need of improvement?
- Which areas will you communicate as the ones in need of future systematic and explicit instruction?

Some key characteristics	Try this for fun with your class . . .
Alphabet recognition	Create a letter–picture sort based on the general interests of the class. For example, recently your class has been excited about an upcoming trip to the local zoo. You've created some picture cards that match the sounds /m/, /s/, /a/, and /t/. As part of the Do-Now, or Think-Now, students work in partnerships to cut out and say and sort the cards.
Blending	Later in this chapter we reference the importance of the vocabulary meeting. Consider leaving some of the words in the meeting blank, creating opportunities for students to string together letter sounds previously taught. Call on a "word blender" in the class to help.
Dictation	Adoniou (2019) reminds us that spelling tests are ineffective. Instead, why not include ungraded opportunities for dictation. Consider the skills that students have been working on in phonics. Then, design a dictation activity for students to capture your thoughts about a character in a recent read-aloud. Pass out the white boards, and engage your students: "Word decoders, are you ready? Let's get started. Here are your two sentences: *Pete the Cat looks good in his new sunglasses. He finds a way to love today!*"
Word awareness	After carefully looking at the interest inventories conducted earlier in the school year, the teacher recognizes that many students play a musical instrument. Some students, however, still struggle with word awareness. The teacher passes out a resealable plastic bag to each of the five groups in the classroom. In the bags, the word *instrument* is cut up. "As part of our activity to get started today, I've noticed that four or five of you in the class share an interest. Build as many words as you can within your small groups. Let's see which group can work their way up to building our 10-letter mystery word."
High-frequency words	In Chapter 5, we reference some word wall games that make for a productive use of the literacy environment. Blevins (2019) reminds us that the top 250–300 words "are generally taught in grades K–2. Past grade 2, when the majority of the high-frequency words have been introduced, students need to be continually assessed on their mastery of these words, as a lack of fluency can impede comprehension" (p. 5). Every moment counts! If you have a few minutes, carve out a class competition and sort the room into two competing lines of students! What a great opportunity to practice phonics prior to lining up for lunch, recess, dismissal, or at other times!

FIGURE 6.5. Sample activities for developing students' phonics skills.

Fun with Fluency

In our early literacy classrooms, we are reminded that, in addition to phonemic awareness and phonics, fluency plays a major role in helping our students become more confident and strategic readers. Students who demonstrate fluency are less likely to experience word identification problems that hinder reading comprehension and are able to read quickly, accurately, automatically, and expressively (Cunningham & Allington, 2015).

Based on its importance, we know that a number of practices top the list in developing students' reading fluency. *Round robin, or popcorn reading, is not one of them.* Over the past few years, we have engaged in discussions with attendees at our presentations or school visits who have buckled down on the excuses far and wide for holding onto this practice:

- "But my students enjoy when I call on them to read aloud. Some of them readily volunteer."
- "How else am I supposed to hear them develop and improve as readers?"

First, it is likely that the students who volunteer are already the confident or more advanced readers in the classroom. Their eagerness to read aloud (resulting in your likely enthusiastic call on the reader) likely stirs up some anxiety in reluctant, or striving readers (or whatever the latest terminology coins students who otherwise struggle and lack confidence). Students who publicly pay more attention to their fluency at the expense of feeling embarrassed in front of their peers are less likely to monitor comprehension and be able to engage in collaborative conversations related to the text.

Lit ☀ Idea

Develop opportunities for students to practice reading for fluency that exist in more supportive environments where the students do not appear to stand out in front of the whole group:

- *Repeated readings*—Provide opportunities for students to revisit and reread familiar texts over the course of a number of days.
- *Echo reading*—Read a sentence or paragraph at a time, and have students model your fluent and expressive reading of the text.
- *Choral reading*—Allow opportunities for students to read texts together as a class (especially about subjects and topics that motivate the students collectively).
- *Readers' theatre*—Gain access to scripts that allow students to practice and perform. Don't have access to the topics you're looking for? Draft your own, or create a shared writing experience for students to collectively write the script.
- *Podcast it!*—Students are more likely to read with increased attention and practice for authentic audiences. If students know that the repeated readings will result in a podcast, they are more likely to rehearse and pay attention to areas such as accuracy, prosody, and rate. Check out Chapter 10 for more ideas related to technology and literacy.

Lindsay Bernero, a literacy support tAeacher (LST) in the Linden Public Schools, advocates for activities such as Fluency Idol, Fluency Fridays, and Fluency Walks. With these activities in mind, encourage your students to have fun reading their favorite books, songs, poems, or other texts as a feature. Showcase these performances on Fridays or on another special day of the week or month. If there are texts that can be segmented, or divided into smaller chunks, type them out on computer paper and create a fluency path around the classroom or school. As students follow the journey, they read in a whisper what's on the paper. For example, in one local park in Bermuda, tourists who walk in the park engage in an entire story of "Tiny the Tree Frog" who explores the beauties of the island of Bermuda (Mulderig, 1992). Visitors to the island enjoy nature walks in a local park in the city of Hamilton, while practicing their fluency as readers in a tropical destination. We can create the same joy for reading in our schools and classrooms.

Lit 💡 Idea

If students are still reading like robots, check out the awesome GoNoodle (2016) entitled *Don't Read Like a Robot* by Blazer Fresh (*www.youtube.com/watch?v=xjtPMiumixA*).

Fostering a Word Nerd Culture: A Focus on Vocabulary

All too often we give in to the other components of literacy instruction at the expense of helping our students develop a robust vocabulary. In addition to the vocabulary ideas presented in earlier chapters, we provide some vocabulary meeting examples that make students' literacy lives central to our literacy teaching. We believe that a joyful and interactive focus on helping students become more independent word learners is worth its weight in gold. The vocabulary meetings listed in Figure 6.6 are planned to include (1) word wall words, (2) Tier Two vocabulary that requires instruction, (3) a think-aloud for introducing the meeting and format, (4) the message itself, and (5) opportunities to scaffold for students' individual literacy needs. In these vocabulary lessons, students are excited to begin a new journey into reading adventure tales that include pirate stories.

While these vocabulary meetings address students' interests in the genre of adventure, there are countless opportunities for us to prioritize students' literacy lives in the curriculum in order to bring forth a passion, interest, and high levels of engagement for learning new words and becoming more proficient readers.

Lit 💡 Idea

Create vocabulary meetings based on (1) the languages spoken at students' homes, (2) the unique facts about students' countries of origin, (3) the traditions and holidays celebrated by your students, (4) the diversity of family arrangements, and (5) the lingering questions that come up as the curriculum is taught over the course of the school year.

DAY 1	
Word wall words (sight words from the text):	*was, the, he, about, want*
Tier Two vocabulary **focus**:	*attic, reveal, lurch, horizon, shipshape*
Think-aloud (connecting to class learning):	"Readers, today I have a vocabulary message to introduce the brand new book we will read this week. Because you have shown a great interest in adventure, you are just going to love our new read-alouds!"
Message (circle one): narrative poem (letter) journal list riddle informational recipe other	Courageous Readers, The sun is on the **horizon** and the ocean waves are **lurching** forward, crashing onto the beach. Can you picture it? We start our adventure today in an **attic** that is **shipshape,** but we won't end there. We follow a boy and his grandad—but what will their adventure **reveal**? Let's read and find out! Mrs. Wilson
Possible scaffolding ideas:	choral reading; echo reading; call kids up to identify words with beginning letter sounds; pausing for punctuation; clapping syllables; reading the message in a different voice
DAY 2	
Word wall words (sight words from the text):	*was, the, he, about, want*
Tier Two vocabulary **focus**:	*attic, reveal, lurch, horizon, shipshape*
Think-aloud (connecting to class learning):	"Readers, before we dive into our book, let's see who our vocabulary message **reveals** to us today. Help your classmates figure out this exciting riddle I created for you!"
Message (circle one): narrative poem letter journal list (riddle) informational recipe other	Who am I? I **lurch** through the **attic,** but don't be scared, for I am only a small animal. I am tiny and quick, with a big bushy tail. When I climb the rafters, I like to sit, eat an acorn, and stare out at the **horizon**. I'm so happy that I chose this attic, it's **shipshape** and so easy to live in. Should I **reveal** who I am? Or can you guess? (*squirrel*)
Possible scaffolding ideas:	choral reading; echo reading; call kids up to identify words with beginning letter sounds; pausing for punctuation; clapping syllables; reading the message in a different voice

(continued)

FIGURE 6.6. Vocabulary meetings.

DAY 3	
Word wall words (sight words from the text):	was, the, he, about, want
Tier Two vocabulary **focus**:	attic, reveal, lurch, horizon, shipshape
Think-aloud (connecting to class learning):	"Readers, before we dive into our book, we have a fun vocabulary poem. You've been learning so many new and exciting vocabulary words this week. Before we begin, turn and talk to your partner about a vocabulary word you know that you didn't know before."
Message (circle one): narrative (poem) letter journal list riddle informational recipe other	First the **attic,** then an island adventure, **Lurching** through the water, on a ship that's **shipshape** arriving on shore. From the sandy beach we can watch the sun rising on the **horizon,** It looks as if the sky has **revealed** a yellow diamond.
Possible scaffolding ideas:	choral reading; echo reading; call kids up to identify words with beginning letter sounds; pausing for punctuation; clapping syllables; reading the message in a different voice
DAY 4	
Word wall words (sight words from the text):	was, the, he, about, want
Tier Two vocabulary **focus**:	attic, reveal, lurch, horizon, shipshape
Think-aloud (connecting to class learning):	"Readers, we have a very special vocabulary message today from our very own main character, Syd."
Message (circle one): narrative poem (letter) journal list riddle informational recipe other	Hi Friends, Syd here! I wanted to write and say thank you for reading my story. I was in my grandad's **attic** yesterday, looking at pictures of us. I sure do miss him! Do you know that his house still looks **shipshape** even with him gone? I stayed in his **attic** until the sun left the **horizon** and, when I got home, my mom **revealed** another letter from grandad! He said that it was about time for me to come visit again. I can't wait to get aboard that old ship and have it **lurch** through the ocean waves all the way to grandad's island. Hey, maybe we'll "*sea*" you there someday! Ahoy, Syd
Possible scaffolding ideas:	choral reading; echo reading; call kids up to identify words with beginning letter sounds; pausing for punctuation; clapping syllables; reading the message in a different voice

(continued)

FIGURE 6.6. *(continued)*

DAY 5	
Word wall words (sight words from the text):	*and, he, make, did, was*
Tier Two vocabulary **focus:**	*pirate, treasure, capture, sail, crew*
Think-aloud (connecting to class learning):	"Readers, let's take a look at our vocabulary message to see if we can guess what our nonfiction book will be about based on our recent adventures."
Message (circle one): narrative poem (letter) journal list riddle informational recipe other	Arrggggg young sailors, Are you ready to **sail** away? Grab your finest **crew** and come aboard the *Queen Anne's Revenge*, a **pirate** ship of the finest kind. While moving across the open waters, keep your eye out for a **treasure** to **capture**. We can enjoy the spoils together! Can you guess what we will be reading about? Mrs. Wilson
Possible scaffolding ideas:	choral reading; echo reading; call kids up to identify words with beginning letter sounds; pausing for punctuation; clapping syllables; reading the message in a different voice
DAY 6	
Word wall words (sight words from the text):	*and, he, make, did, was*
Tier Two vocabulary **focus:**	*pirate, treasure, capture, sail, crew*
Think-aloud (connecting to class learning):	"Readers, today's vocabulary message comes right from Blackbeard's ship, the *Queen Anne's Revenge*. One of his to-do lists is to give us an idea of a day in the life of a pirate. Let find out how pirates live their daily lives."
Message (circle one): narrative poem letter journal (list) riddle informational recipe other	<u>**Pirate**</u> To-Do List 1. **Sail** with the winds. 2. Have the **crew** mop the deck. 3. **Capture** Captain Jack Sparrow. 4. Find **treasure**!
Possible scaffolding ideas:	choral reading; echo reading; call kids up to identify words with beginning letter sounds; pausing for punctuation; clapping syllables; reading the message in a different voice

FIGURE 6.6. *(continued)*

Ditch the Reading Logs: A Second Glance at Independent Reading

As much as vocabulary suffers at the expense of other core literacy components, we stumble into classrooms where dreadful reading logs are still robbing the joy for reading one reader and book at a time. In the infographic in Figure 6.7, we offer some alternatives based on the work of our colleagues and the research base at large.

Lit 💡 Idea

Writing for authentic purposes: Create a book challenge within your classroom related to some of the grade-level favorites. Introduce a dialogic journal for students and their families to share their personal reactions to the texts. Include one to two pages in the journal for each text that will be shared from your lending library.

Something I Found Worth Talking About
(quote, sentence, passage, paragraph, visual, etc.)

Our Reaction
(We think . . . , When we read this . . . , We discussed . . . , etc.)

CONCLUSION

In this chapter, we begin with the premise that joy and happiness have to take center stage in our literacy lives, especially as they relate to the early literacy classroom. From there, we need to embrace the reading foundational skills that help our students become more tactful and confident readers. As we do so, we should approach such topics with collaboration and civility, centering joy for students over our own personal interests, beliefs, or biases. Phonological awareness, phonemic awareness, fluency, vocabulary, reading comprehension, writing, engagement, and motivation are all key (as expressed throughout the book), but they also have different seats on the school bus when it comes to prioritizing students' needs. Some students will wait for quite a few stops before they depart at the corner of phonemic awareness and phonics, whereas others will enter our classrooms beyond ready to proceed to stops further down the line. Find joy in helping your readers and writers discover their strengths. Be bold, and be willing to break the mold of traditional weekly spelling tests and reading logs if they are part of the norm. Be a literacy changemaker, and be fearless in pursuit of ensuring that students are at (or doggonit) as close to proficiency as possible by the end of their emergent/early years of literacy development.

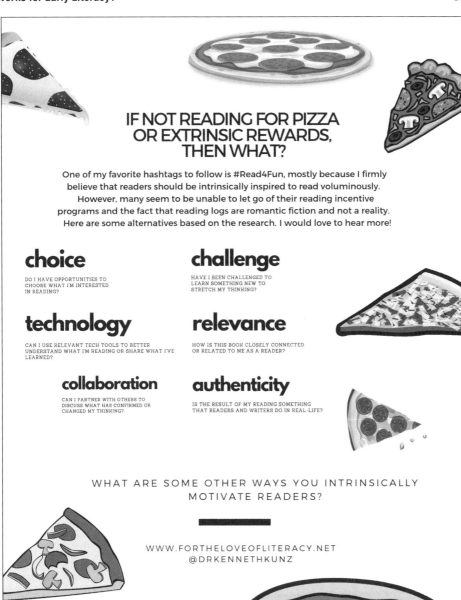

FIGURE 6.7. Suggested alternatives to reading for extrinsic motivators.

Stop, Think, and Take Action

Based on the ideas presented in this chapter on early literacy, take time to consider the ways in which you might recalibrate the literacy program in your classroom or school community. Reflect on the following:

If your role is that of a . . .

- **Classroom teacher** or **teacher-leader**—Administer the interest inventory introduced at the beginning of the chapter. Find trends: What brings *your* students joy? Now, where will these topics appear when developing students' phonemic awareness, phonics, fluency, vocabulary, comprehension, and writing?

- **Literacy specialist** or **literacy coach**—Based on the ideas presented in the chapter, what area is an "easy" win for further developing the strengths of the readers you work with? What's one practice that can be seamlessly implemented into the intervention schedule for helping students who need that extra dose of literacy instruction daily?

- **School administrator** or **school-level leader**—We know that the work of teachers in early literacy classrooms is worthwhile, but also demanding. Consider asking your teachers what would make their school year easier or more joyful. These solutions are often not all that costly, but demonstrate to teachers that they are respected and valued by the building leader.

- **District administrator** or **district-level leader**—Funds often exist for early literacy and innovative programs that engage families and communities. Identify the successful programs that resulted in high levels of family engagement in your school or district community. What areas need improvement? Seek the assistance of a respected professional developer or college/university literacy faculty member in your region to brainstorm ideas.

- **Professional developer**—Resources such as *Literacy Development in the Early Years: Helping Children Read and Write* (Morrow, 2020), now in its ninth edition, are available. What's introduced that's new? Create a survey for the early literacy teachers and administrators in the local school community. Have participants rank what they would like to learn more about, from most important to less important.

CHAPTER 7

Recalibrating Literacy Programs
What Works for Adolescent Learners?

Last, we have to have the courage to lead in our classrooms, in our schools, and in our communities as we commit to developing readers, writers, and thinkers who possess empathy and power. At the center of all this for me is a sign I read at the Save Our Schools March in Washington, D.C., in July 2011: *Nothing without joy.*
—PENNY KITTLE

The literacy changemakers at Hatchery Hill realize that student motivation and engagement are increased when joyful learning takes place in classrooms, even as the research suggests that motivation and engagement are more challenging to address in the upper grades. The team understands the important role that vocabulary, comprehension, and writing play with students at this level. Mrs. Griffin is inspired by suggestions from Mrs. Schiano and Mrs. Rosenfeld to begin a schoolwide focus on vocabulary. Beyond a simple "word of the week," they would like to encourage everyone in the school community to get excited about word learning. Mrs. Calabrese provides a professional text for the team and teachers at Hatchery Hill to read and discuss voluntarily. The team meets to discuss a plan for implementation, starting with a kickoff day for teachers and students.

READING ON THE DECLINE

According to the Scholastic (2019a) Reading Report, reading for enjoyment and viewpoints that recognize the importance of reading both decline sharply after age 8 (see Figure 7.1). Some critics believe that this decline is due to the fact that students' attention is diverted by competing forces like video games and social media, and the fact that parents often decide to stop reading aloud to their children at this age. "Frequent readers" ages 12–17 read an average of 39 books per year, whereas infrequent

1. Children who read the most will always outperform children who don't read much.
2. Many studies, including the NAEP (U.S. Department of Education, 2001), have found consistent, positive relationships between pages read and academic performance.
3. Voluminous reading is more important to academic performance than parents' socioeconomic background.
4. Readers are more likely to succeed in the workplace and are more likely to attend college.
5. Reading books is the only out-of-school activity for 16-year-olds that is linked to getting a managerial or professional job later in life (University of Oxford, 2011).
6. Daily reading habits boost the likelihood of students' voting in elections, volunteering for charities, and supporting the arts (National Endowment for the Arts, 2007).
7. Readers of fiction are more empathetic (Chiaet, 2013).

Reading is a predictor of success at life, and may be one of the most effective ways to leverage social change.

FIGURE 7.1. Reasons why we should care about the reading decline after age 8.

readers read an average of 4 books per year. As television consumption rises and reading for enjoyment falls, the same trends are noted in standardized testing across the grades. Here are some startling facts:

- The average college graduate reads only one book per year.
- Less than 1% of the population of the United States reads a newspaper.

In the following sections of this chapter, we advocate for practices that we believe establish joy in reading and support the needs of our adolescent learners.

FALLING IN LOVE WITH WORDS: DON'T FORGET VOCABULARY

Research shows that reading comprehension is dependent upon the meaning readers give words. Therefore, students who possess a stronger vocabulary not only improve their ability to comprehend, but also their ability to communicate through listening, speaking, and writing. In the calendar example from the Wall Intermediate School in Wall, New Jersey, shown in Figure 7.2, a strong emphasis is placed on the use of an extensive vocabulary across content areas. Started by Dr. Ken Kunz as a schoolwide book study of *Word Nerds: Teaching All Students to Learn and Love Vocabulary* (Overturf, Montgomery, & Smith, 2013) a change in culture was experienced when all teachers began to embrace the joy that word learning brings to classrooms. What started as a "Word Nerd Wednesday," during which teachers could wear jeans and a vocabulary T-shirt in support of word learning, evolved into a passion project wherein teachers and students actively participated in vocabulary learning every day.

Monday		
Introduction	**Activity**	**Interactive bulletin board**
Morning announcements: • The word of the week is identified. • A student-friendly definition is provided.	Students are invited to tweet the supervisor of instruction using a special school hashtag for vocabulary. Students are encouraged to use the word in a content-specific sentence with context clues (e.g., #joyfulwordnerds).	The vocabulary word is placed on a bulletin board with a student-friendly definition.
Tuesday		
Morning announcements: • Students are reminded about the word of the week along with the student-friendly definition. • A few student examples submitted via Twitter are shared.	Select the best synonym that matches the word of the week using the poll feature on Twitter.	A few student sentences are featured on the bulletin board.
Wednesday		
Morning announcements: • Students are reminded about the word of the week, and synonyms are provided.	Select the best antonym that is the opposite of the word of the week using the poll feature on Twitter.	Place a list of synonyms on the board.
Thursday		
Morning announcements: • Students are reminded about the word of the week, and antonyms are provided.	Tweet the root of the word using the vocabulary hashtag (e.g., #joyfulwordnerds).	Place a list of antonyms on the board.
Friday		
Morning Announcements: • Students are reminded about the word of the week, and the root of the word is explained.	Students can choose one of the words on the Twitter poll, voting for next week's word. The word with the highest percentage of votes becomes the word for next week.	Place the root of the word on the board.

FIGURE 7.2. A sample vocabulary schedule refined by Matt Kukoda, Supervisor of Intermediate Instruction.

Lit ☀ Idea

Interactive bulletin board spaces in common areas can spark excitement in a school community, especially as adults and children in the building notice that an area has been changed or brightly beautified. Consider designing an area that brings Tier Two vocabulary to the forefront. These interactive spaces can highlight vocabulary, engage both teachers and learners, and allow them to notice the value of the highlighted practice.

A middle school hallway display proudly proclaims that vocabulary words are on their way.

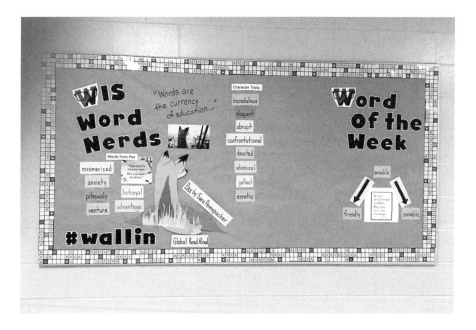

Later, the board becomes a collaborative space with words from a schoolwide read-aloud, a list of character traits, and synonyms.

SUPPORTING READERS WITH SUSTAINED ENGAGEMENT

A few practical tips guide the ways in which we can help students monitor progress toward achieving authentic goals. First, we have to help our students keep track of their reading stamina, noting the roadblocks and hazards that get in the way, and finding solutions to overcome such obstacles. As adults, we recognize those moments that knock us off our balance, but find ways to get back on track. For example, many school teachers admit to "binge-reading" over the summer to make up for the lost time during the school year. Rather than encouraging students to complete meaningless reading logs to, in many cases, forge proof that independent reading took place at home, we should emphasize the importance of what Mary Ehrenworth calls "reading as much as humanly possible." If a student is committed to after-school sports 3 days a week, the remaining 4 days should be dedicated to time set aside to read for pleasure, a right mentioned earlier in the text.

Teachers must keep track of students' reading stamina and whether or not they are engaging with books over an extended period of time. Part of accomplishing this task entails allowing time for students to read in school. Our independent reading advocate and colleague Donalyn Miller reminds us that it's the players who train harder than the coaches in athletics. Therefore, we find joy in visiting classrooms where students are engaged in reading for pleasure and spending more time lost in a book rather than listening to direct instruction from an endless lecture.

Lit 💡 Idea

Encourage your students to try new genres, but if they're "hooked" on a specific genre, help them find the next book in the series. Many students will need help progressing across book ladders. A student who is obsessed with the _____ should be encouraged to move onto the next rung when that series is complete. For example, students may be led to book taste samples from the _____ series. Students need our help in finding their next best read.

Suggested Websites for Choosing Books

- *www.whatshouldIreadnext.com*—includes recommendations based on favorite authors and titles.
- *www.yournextread.com*—a visual website that allows students and teachers to search book jackets.
- *www.readkiddoread.com*—a website created by James Patterson.
- *www.guysread.com*—a website created by Jon Scieszka geared toward boys' interests.

Book Clubs

A wonderful way to capitalize on the terrific new young adult literature now available and to add independent reading time to our students' day is to create book clubs in your classroom. Reading is such an important habit to encourage. It has been proven to increase the ability to focus, improve memory, reduce stress, and develop critical thinking, not to mention that reading serves as a lifelong source of entertainment. When integrated into a well-run literacy class, book clubs can intensify the joy of reading. Who doesn't want to share with a friend the joy of having read a spectacular book?

The teacher's work in setting up book clubs is front-loaded. We must decide:

- the book genre, topic, theme, or author;
- who works well with whom (and who might not work well together);
- the reading levels of our children (to offer everyone books they can handle);
- books that will "speak to" our students (we're hoping to create a love of reading here);
- how long kids will work on a book; and
- how frequently book clubs should happen during the year.

So the first question facing us is: How do we choose book club texts? One good suggestion is to begin by asking our current students to vote for their own favorite reads or to run a "book tasting." We can also look at lists of current award winners, check out what the American Library Association recommends, or ask for help on social media. It's a good idea to offer books on several reading levels and with diverse heroes, since we hope to entice all of our readers.

It's so important that teachers introduce each book with enthusiasm. We're "selling" books here! In great classrooms across the country, teachers conduct book talks daily. Their desire is for their children to hear about as many wonderful books as possible. A book talk can be as simple as what Scholastic Books calls "a book, a hook, and a quick look" (see Figure 7.3). It can be as detailed as we have time for. When we introduce the books (have approximately eight on hand) we may choose to talk a bit about the author, the main character, or an interesting setting. We'll want to read

---

1. Write a quick and captivating summary of the text.
2. Highlight the major themes.
3. Suggest the type of reader who might enjoy the plot.
4. Discuss the author's motivation for publishing the text.
5. Check if there are any captivating book reviews or student-made book trailers that can be accessed.
6. Read from an especially beautiful or exciting part of the text.

FIGURE 7.3. How to give a book talk ("a book, a hook, and a quick look").

a passage from a particularly beautiful, interesting, or controversial part of the book, or from its opening chapter to allow readers to respond to the author's voice. We may also include little hints that might gently guide students to choose books appropriate to their abilities. We might note about one book that the chapters are rather short or mention the page count in the book. For another text we might say, "Wow! There are lots of great, new vocabulary words in this one."

The International Literacy Association expresses its belief in book tastings or "speed dating" of books to increase student engagement (International Literacy Association, 2018a). We want our kids to have whole lists of books they're excited about getting to next. We can organize a display of new book arrivals and leave a note with some tantalizing highlights inside the book for its first reader, which is a wonderful way to spark joy in reading. We can use, or have children use, Flipgrid to record a convincing book talk video to share with others in the form of "If you loved _____, you must read _____." With all of that said, teacher introductions are another form of "book blessings." When the teacher holds up a certain book (or seven or eight of them) and says, "You're going to love this book," that recommendation alone is enticing to our kids. Even if a child chooses a book that is a bit above or below her reading achievement score, the desire to read that particular book and the support of the group can make huge differences. We want to allow children choice; it's highly motivating. It is not the purpose of a book club to tell a child that she may not read a certain book. Her own motivation could make her work harder.

Ask students to rank the books, and tell them that you will try to match them with their first or second choice, but do not give them a guarantee. A good-sized group is from three to five students; above that number, conversation becomes difficult. It is possible, of course, that more than one small group will read the same book. There's a little more work to be done before books are handed out. It's a great idea to create book club toolboxes made from plastic boxes that contain everything a group might need when they're reading. Some basic materials to include are:

- sticky notes (you can never have too many!),
- pencils,
- erasers,
- tape,
- index cards, and
- rulers (to isolate lines).

We also need to discuss both teachers' and students' expectations. For example, noise levels might need to be set. Readers need to know that they are expected to take part in group discussions. Children also should be asked to verbalize what they expect. Are they bored, nervous, or concerned about talking in a group? Addressing these expectations before clubs begin sets the stage for success. Lack of clarity is a sure predictor of trouble down the road. Fisher, Frey, and Hattie (2016) stress that children should be able to ask and answer the following questions about each lesson:

- "What am I learning today [in a mini-lesson or in a group]?"
- "Why am I learning this?"
- "How will I know that I have learned it?"

These questions imply that teachers and students should be aware of the learning intention of each lesson and chapter and their relevance to them as learners. Teachers and children can work together to determine the success criteria.

No matter how good a job of introducing books we have done, it is always possible that a student may approach us after a few days wishing to abandon her book. Both teachers and students should know that this is okay. We don't want to have children stuck reading books they don't love. As teachers, however, we need to monitor progress and make sure that students are not serially abandoning. Have a plan for the possibility that a child may need to abandon a book. Share your "change your book" date beforehand (usually no more than 3 days from the start of reading).

Lit 💡 Idea

Be sure to use reading conference forms to ask students (1) why they have selected the text they are reading, (2) how far along they are in the book, and (3) what information they can recall about what has been read. Be sure that the student is not constantly abandoning and starting new books. If you come across a student who is always on Chapter 1, you may want to help him or her find a better fit based on interest inventories or other considerations.

Sometimes it's the nitty-gritty that trips up a book club. Teachers may want to give each child a folder with a couple of pockets to hold the calendar (created by each group to determine how many pages need to be read each day), possible discussion questions, a "talk moves" sheet, a vocabulary bookmark, their reader's notebook, and whatever other handouts the teacher has deemed helpful. Each group could have a different-colored folder to help with organization. Everyone knows that, on book club days, they are responsible for having their folder, their book, and a pencil at the ready. When we're prepared to take part in a book club discussion, we're much more likely to find it enjoyable.

Lit 💡 Idea

Allow group members to choose a club name (e.g., Born to Read, Reading Is Lit!, LitPositive) and encourage them to create a group constitution, touching on the responsibilities and joys of reading and keeping up to date with group norms.

Independent Reading

Personally, we find that there is great joy for us on a day when we know we can look forward to having lots of time to read books of our own choosing. We can instill that same enjoyment in adolescents when we allow them time to do independent reading. Penny Kittle (2013) makes the following statement, and we agree with her. "I believe in the power of guiding student choice to increase engagement, skill, and joy" (p. xiv). She argues that our children have a need to own their reading, much as writing teachers are taught that students need to own their writing. If, however, they do not regularly practice reading, they will not build the stamina necessary to read the classics, or books that English teachers often require them to read. Giving students time to read in class, a choice of which texts to read, and talking with them about the books they are reading are what allow them to become voracious readers: people who read with joy. Meeting children where they are, and helping them set goals for books they enjoy is the starting point.

Lit 💡 Idea

Check out some additional great ideas in Kimberly Cockley's (2016) article "Joy in Reading: A Middle School Literacy Enrichment Program."

We all know students who struggle to understand what they read; indeed, we all know readers who struggle, period. If reading is confusing to us, it is certainly not pleasurable. Kittle suggests that those readers have neither the capacity for reading (stamina), nor the capacity for working through frustration, which takes time to develop. She has found through her work with high school students that asking children to read books that are too difficult for them is a problem. The solution for her own classes has been to increase the volume of books they are reading first, while building skills and conferring with them, and later introducing more challenging material. It is that balance between pleasure and challenge, along with individual goal setting, that allows children to begin to develop a reading habit.

John Guthrie (2008) reminds us that humans tend to pursue interests for their own sakes. He suggests that identifying the intrinsic interests of adolescents and allowing them to research and study those interests can be highly motivating. His thoughts coalesce around what he calls a *passion project*. Passion projects are written works for which students are given the following directions:

- Identify a topic about which you are passionate.
- Write about that topic.
- Read a novel of your choice on the topic.
- Create a connection to your topic (art work, photo essay).
- Present your topic to reveal your passion (p. 91).

Although Guthrie's approach was originally designed for multilingual learners (see Chapter 8 for more information about this population), it makes sense that all students could benefit from and enjoy working under these conditions. We have seen these projects assigned with slightly different directions to students in grades 6–10 with much success. Bringing joy and engagement to any assignment makes the work both more worthwhile and more satisfying.

STEP INTO THE CLASSROOM OF NICOLE MANCINI, MIDDLE SCHOOL LITERACY TEACHER

In the following sections, Nicole Mancini, a fifth-grade literacy teacher at Bedminster Township School in Bedminster, New Jersey, shares her observations and recommendations for engaging students with reading and promoting a lifelong love of books.

Video games. Friends. Sports. Television. You name it, and there's a distraction. That's why when it comes to student engagement and motivation, educators need to pull out all the stops. Our students are living during a time of heightened awareness about "self" and trying to navigate between who they truly are and how they appear to their peers. Even the youngest in our classrooms pick up on social cues that can affect their willingness to try new things and embrace those that they already love. In terms of literacy, this can be the difference between a child becoming a joyful lifelong reader or not. As a result, we must find new ways to excite our students about reading.

When educators ask me how I motivate my students to read, my answer is simple: read the books they're reading. In doing so, you'll discover a world much different from the adult texts that populate coffee tables in most homes. When you choose books that students love and combine it with the ease and accessibility of social media, you can create connections with authors quite easily. Most authors want to hear from teachers and kids and are often willing to collaborate on activities. This, in turn, can lead to endless possibilities for your students.

Author Visits

As discussed earlier, book talks are a great influence on students. They are like movie previews and can have an immediate effect on a child's willingness to read. To take this a step further, author visits provide a more personal connection. Imagine hooking your students on a text during a book club, an interactive read-aloud, or independent reading, and then inviting the author in to talk about the book further—the motivations behind plot elements, the inner workings of a character's brain, the process it took to bring the story to life! Students are enthralled to hear the "behind the scenes" details that helped create the book. I have seen even the most disengaged readers light up and actually go back to interact with the text again as a result of an author's visit. Others have gone on to read different books by the same author or even written complimentary stories. Some even take it upon themselves to explore the genre and find new books to enjoy. This one-on-one time between students and writers truly makes an impact.

Virtual Visits

Because financial constraints can limit the possibility of in-person visits, a wide variety of authors also offer free virtual sessions via Skype, Google Hangouts, and Zoom. Many authors already have information about virtual visits on their websites. You can also research who is available through the Microsoft in Education—Skype in the Classroom page online as well as Kate Messner's World Read Aloud Day listing. Don't be afraid to reach out to an author through Twitter or Instagram. That is how I actually got started with my Skype sessions, and I haven't looked back since. Every other month, my students get to interact with an author as a result.

Consider these options:

- *Book clubs*. Before or after students read; during club meetings.
- *Read-alouds*. Celebrate World Read Aloud Day each February with an author session; ask authors to read parts of their books as they imagined them.
- *Book talks*. Ask authors to tell students about their current and upcoming books.
- *Writing*. Discussions of the writing process or strategies; have students share their stories to get feedback.
- *Career exploration*. Authors can share their daily life and struggles; students can ask questions.

However you decide to incorporate a virtual visit, please keep in mind that although a vast majority of authors embrace it, not all authors are willing or able to offer virtual visits. If someone you reach out to is unavailable, don't push the issue, and instead move on to someone else. Remember that most authors do virtual visits on a volunteer basis, offering time that otherwise would be spent writing. While orchestrating an online visit might seem imitating because of the technology aspect, don't let this get in your way. Ask your school's technology teacher or director to show you the ropes; it is quite simple and can really engage and motivate your students. It also fosters a human connection as students see the person behind the name. Similarly, using a diverse group of authors allows kids to connect on a much deeper level, as they actually see authors who look and sound like them.

A middle school hallway proudly displays inclusive wall art designed by Isabel Casais, a student.

Social Connections

As the school year progresses and activities like the ones discussed are implemented, keep the momentum going by sharing pictures, drawings, poems, stories, thoughts, and more, with authors on social media. They love to see them! Recently, an author popular among my fifth graders had emergency surgery. One student felt such a connection to her books that she actually designed, wrote, and illustrated a multipage graphic novel for her and asked me to send it. I was overcome by her kindness and willingness to go above and beyond for someone she had only met through stories. It is these connections that can be so powerful in our classrooms, so encourage your students to express their thoughts or ask questions; take what they produce and post it on social media, and you'll often get immediate feedback from the author. Asking the class to share with writers via social media—once more—makes them seem more human instead of these out-of-reach beings we only know through the bio in a book.

I have been fortunate enough to leverage the power of social media to create a unique atmosphere in my fifth-grade classroom. Each year, students come to me with varying degrees of engagement with reading; my job is to harness whatever means are available to bring it to new levels. Thankfully, Twitter has been my magic wand in achieving these deeper ties. The connections I have formed with published authors and educators over the Internet have been powerful and quite honestly led to me revitalizing my career at a time when burnout was on the horizon. I encourage educators to reach beyond the four walls of their classrooms and explore ways they can forge relationships with authors. It will truly change your teaching and make an impact on students for a lifetime.

Lit 💡 Idea

Make reading a "social" event for students, giving them the same excitement they get from other forms of media.

CONCLUSION

Adolescents have vastly different literacy needs than elementary school children. Although teachers can introduce their own favorite texts to their younger students, the same approach may not work with middle schoolers. It becomes more and more important to know and tap into students' interests, to use content that is relevant to them, to make learning enjoyable when possible, to offer choices, and to know the needs of the group of students sitting in front of us.

Adolescents have a desire to feel significant. If they can make a connection between what is personally important to them and the task at hand, they will work more willingly. Developmentally, teenagers are in the throes of deciding who they are and how to separate themselves from who they are "supposed to be." Therefore, allowing some degree of choice in an assignment is another way to motivate these students.

If our students are struggling to begin an assignment, perhaps they need help knowing how to start what may seem like a very big job. Helping them to think through the process or breaking the task up into smaller, achievable parts may help. At times just giving students a copy of a calendar can allow them to see that smaller deadlines exist within a long-term project. It makes the goal feel more achievable.

Lit 💡 Idea

Some of our favorite hashtags on Twitter that address social justice and equity for our adolescent learners are:

> #OwnVoices
> #ProjectLitCommunity
> #WeNeedMoreDiverseBooks

Follow these hashtags to become introduced to great resources, professional texts, and communities for advocating on behalf of all learners.

Allowing children to fail as long as they are on the road to success helps them to learn that all growth and success are based on previous (and possibly failing) attempts. It's okay, and even important, to experience failure; the key is to continue to rise to the challenge.

All of us work better when an element of fun is introduced, and teenagers are certainly no exception to this rule. If they can listen to music as they work, play a game to learn a new skill, use technology to solve a problem, or reach out to crowd-source it via Twitter or other social media, students are usually motivated to work longer and harder. As we worked on the creation of this book, the best times were when we worked together, enjoying each other's company.

Stop, Think, and Take Action

Based on the ideas presented in this chapter on what works for adolescents, take time to consider the ways in which you might add your expertise to motivate and engage those students. Reflect on the following:

If your role is that of a . . .

- **Classroom teacher** or **teacher-leader**—Ask yourself, "Do I keep the interests of my students in mind as I choose texts? Is there a way I might be able to 'let go of the reins' in my classroom for a bit to allow for student choice?" Start small, with just one book or assignment choice.
- **Literacy specialist** or **literacy coach**—Ask yourself, "Am I keeping up to date on culturally relevant texts? Am I reminding teachers who are sticking to the 'canon' that they might be able to designate time or space to substitute another novel, but still teach the theme they had planned?"
- **School administrator** or **school-level leader**—Ask yourself, "Can I free up money from my school budget to help teachers replenish their libraries and build more socially

relevant spaces? In what other ways can I assist teachers who are willing to take the risk of adding to the canon, and how can I help convince others to join this group?"

- **District administrator** or **district-level leader**—Look at the trends in your data and identify communities of adolescent learners who would benefit from personalized reading communities. For example, if middle school boys are not achieving levels of proficiency, engage the literacy team in designing a fun and student-centered opportunity for students to choose books and collaborate in unique ways.

- **Professional developer**—Ask yourself, "How can I help teachers and lead them to use newer, more relevant, and diverse material? Can I model lessons using new award-winning novels? Am I keeping in mind the fact that both students and teachers need to build stamina and frustration tolerance?"

CHAPTER 8

"Eyes Lit Up with Joy"
Advocating for Multilingual Learners

To learn a language is to have one more window
from which to look at the world.
— CHINESE PROVERB

The administration and faculty at Hatchery Hill have noticed a steady increase of multilingual learners within their school community. While invigorated by the influx of diversity and a global perspective, the team feels compelled to equip themselves with the best language-learning strategies, not just in their ESL classrooms but in all their classrooms, in an effort to provide the appropriate avenues to second-language success. Mrs. Griffin is conscious of the fact that she can help the faculty and staff implement literacy strategies, as well as modifications and accommodations for literacy instruction, in a manner that will not overwhelm the teachers, but instead furnish them with the tools to aid in the development of second-language acquisition within their classrooms. Mrs. Rosenfeld provides support by saying, "As a coach, I can offer the teachers my support in real time by modeling different vocabulary and/or comprehension activities that will be helpful in classrooms with multilingual learners." She immediately reaches out to her supervisor, Mrs. Calabrese, for suggestions related to professional reading on this topic. Excitement is already building, as Mrs. DeMarco is the first teacher to sign up for in-class modeled lessons.

ESTABLISHING AN ASSET MINDSET

Regardless of where you are as you read this book, it's likely that you have been impacted in some way by the growing number of students who do not speak English as their first language. Over the years, this population has been referred to in different ways, including English language learners (ELLs) and English learners (ELs). The authors agree with the latest designation bestowed upon this group, which is multilingual learners (MLLs). This term embraces the asset mindset that helps us find and share joy in the instruction of our multilingual students. Rather than adopting the deficit mindset, focusing on the lack of English proficiency, we focus on the fact that these students and their families are working to become multilingual. When considering that the majority of the world's population is either bilingual or multilingual, we find that monolingualism is the exception rather than the norm (Valdés, n.d.). With that in mind, students working to attain English language proficiency are in the midst of a difficult and exciting journey, and it is one to be supported and celebrated!

As described by the National Center for Education Statistics (2019), "The percentage of public school students in the United States who were ELLs was higher in fall 2016 (9.6 percent, or 4.9 million students) than in fall 2000 (8.1 percent, or 3.8 million students)." The increasing number of MLLs means so many wonderful things for our public schools: increasing diversity, an increasing global perspective, and an increasing exposure to different languages. MLLs have so much to offer our classrooms, and they should never be looked at as being a deficit, but rather as being an asset.

The work of Tonya Ward Singer brings the asset mindset to the forefront in her book *EL Excellence Every Day: The Flip-to Guide for Differentiating Academic Literacy* (2018). With an asset mindset, we see what the student has. With a deficit mindset, we see what the student does not have. Valuing the students' assets, priorities, and needs alongside our expectations of excellence for all learners is how we're going to create joyful learning opportunities for this incredibly important and often disadvantaged population of students.

The authors fully embrace the asset mindset and encourage you to keep it at the core of your work with your MLLs. When setting goals, discuss the student's assets with him to help determine where he needs to go next. When designing lessons and activities, keep the student's assets in mind to capitalize on the success and confidence that he feels, while encouraging him to take risks. Embodying the asset mindset in all you do will lead you to find great joy in the eyes and smiles of students who are proud and feel successful, and this, we promise, will bring you joy as an educator as you watch your students grow and flourish.

FOSTERING A WELCOMING SENSE OF BELONGING FOR MULTILINGUAL LEARNERS

Picture it: Your class is quickly learning all the routines and procedures without any hiccups, you have completed all the beginning-of-the year benchmark assessments for each student, and you have been blessed with the "perfect schedule." The school year is off to a great start. You head home for the weekend, happy as a lark, on that first Friday in October, and when you return on Monday, your principal greets you with a student who has just enrolled, "does not speak any English," and has been placed in your class. Although most teachers would start to panic upon hearing this news, not you. You made the wise decision to read this book, and will be able to ensure that your multilingual learner feels as welcome in your classroom as every other student! The suggestions below will cultivate an environment of welcomeness and take into account the application of multiple theories to advocate for quality instruction for MLLs.

Partner Up!

Partner your new multilingual learner with a buddy from your class, perhaps one who changes weekly or monthly. This student-buddy will be the designated helper to the multilingual learner in your classroom as well as when they set out to navigate the school. This pairing will do two things: allow your multilingual learner to feel more accepted and comfortable in her new school and allow the student-buddy to feel a sense of responsibility, which most children crave. Win, win! An important word of caution: the responsibility of helping MLLs should not be stressful or take away from English-speaking students' learning experiences. If you notice that your English speakers are missing instruction because they are helping to explain something to their multilingual peers, it's time to add some additional scaffolds to your instruction. We want learning to be equitable and fair for everyone.

Use Pictures!

A picture tells a thousand words. In addition to providing pictures in your daily instruction, it's equally important to have visual aids posted around your classroom. When introducing new or even familiar topics that may be unfamiliar to your MLLs, display pictures to help them make connections and develop background knowledge.

Use Videos!

If a picture tells a thousand words, think about how powerful a video could be. A great strategy is to show a video to the entire class (bonus points if there are captions or written words incorporated) when introducing a new concept or building background knowledge. Then, make the video available on your class website or on Google Classroom for your students to view whenever they need a refresher or if they want to review the concept independently.

Talk with Your Hands!

Using your hands counts as a visual aid. Miming words as you speak them, often referred to as *total physical response,* will help your MLLs to make sense of what you're saying. Pointing to your visuals or to important words as you discuss them will help your students make connections between ideas, objects, and language.

Immerse Your Students!

People like to vacation on islands; they do not like to *be* islands. Please do not isolate your MLLs by having them work on a task that is completely different from the rest of your class. Please do not exclude them from class discussions, even if your intentions are to create a less stressful environment or decrease anxiety. Your MLLs feel isolated enough by not having adequate communication skills in English to traverse the school day. When we include them in discussions, even if they are not expected to actively participate, we are providing opportunities for them to improve their listening skills in English, which is an important hurdle in the development of English language proficiency. When in doubt, immerse, immerse, immerse! MLLs acquire so much more when they are fully immersed in their learning environments rather than being isolated from them.

Lit 💡 Idea

Don't confine books of other languages to just the world language classroom. Bring in bilingual stories for all your students to enjoy. In a conscious effort to cultivate a global perspective and second-language acquisition, a classroom teacher in New Jersey read aloud a bilingual story to her second-grade classroom. By reading the story a second time in Spanish, she showed her Spanish-speaking students that she recognized their language as equally important. Moreover, it empowered her MLLs by putting them in positions to assist English-speaking students with vocabulary translations and comprehension of the story—a scenario they didn't find themselves in often! To acknowledge all the languages in your classroom is to acknowledge all the students in your classroom.

Getting to Know the Student behind the "Label"

As explored in Chapter 2, the best thing a teacher can do is get to know his or her students. The second best thing a teacher can do is allow for the students to get to know each other.

- *Culture-based "getting to know you" activities*—These can include examining the languages you or your family speak and the country where you were born and/or country where your parents or grandparents were born. When you allow students to have a platform to learn about one another and talk about themselves and the people that matter most to them—their family—it sends the message that you care about who they are as individuals, and we all know that students learn a great deal more from people they feel care about them.
- *Guess Who? (the class version)*—Students have to provide answers to basic "getting to know you" questions, such as how many siblings students have, whether they have pets, and what their favorite food or color might be. The class then works to match the answers with the correct students. This could even be a fun first-week-of-school activity and could be repeated a month or two later as the students learn more about one another. Make sure you play, too. Students love to learn about their teacher!

Representation Matters: Centering Multilingual Voices in the Curriculum

Think about your classroom library. Even better, put this book down, and go take a good look at your texts. Are all of your students represented? If all of your students are represented, are there characters and stories that will introduce your students to people who are different from them? In her seminal essay, "Mirrors, Windows, and Sliding Glass Doors," Rudine Sims Bishop (1990) explains the importance of providing texts to readers that allow them to see themselves in the books—not just as background characters but as heroes, heroines, and protagonists who experience life in ways your students can connect to and appreciate. She profoundly states:

> Literature transforms human experience and reflects it back to us, and in that reflection we can see our own lives and experiences as part of the larger human experience. Reading, then, becomes a means of self-affirmation, and readers often seek mirrors in their books. . . . When children cannot find themselves in the books they read, or when the images they see are distorted, negative, or laughable, they learn a powerful lesson about how they are devalued in the society of which they are a part. Our classrooms need to be places where all children from all the cultures that make up the salad bowl of American society can find their mirrors. (p. ix)

The importance of assembling a library that is representative of various cultures cannot be overstated. Not only is it important for your multilingual students to see themselves reflected in books, it is important for all of your students to see accurate and positive representations of people who look like them—and of people who *don't* look like them. If your students "live in a bubble," pop it! When they leave the comfort of their school environment, they will meet people of all shapes, sizes, and colors. They should be well prepared before that point to approach any of those people with understanding and without bias, and stocking your classroom library with diverse characters is one small but necessary step toward that goal.

Lit 💡 Idea

Let the students hear and see different languages around the classroom. One Spanish-speaking classroom teacher often uses Spanish words to compliment her first graders. Another teacher incorporates the idea of compliment cards and titled them "Compliment to My Compañero/a," or "Compliment to My Partner."

One teacher's compliment card.

Empowering the Families of Multilingual Learners: Bringing Joy Home

It is vitally important to invite our MLLs' families to participate in the school community (additional ideas related to family literacy are shared in Chapter 9). There are so many different ways to include these families and help them understand the vital role they play not only in their children's lives but in the school community as a whole. Participation at the school may be limited for these families owing to their cultural norms or their own hesitancy, so reaching out to them must be considered and approached with care. Building trust with families over time will help to create an environment in which families not only feel comfortable attending and participating in school events, but also in which they know that they, as well as their languages and their cultures, are valued. The following ideas will get you started, but once you get to know your multilingual families, you can use your own resourcefulness—and theirs!—to create events that meet their needs and celebrate their cultures.

- *Whenever possible, send communication to parents in their home language.* This is required by many states and also by the U. S. Department of Education, as set forth in its "Dear Colleague Letter" (U.S. Department of Education, Office of Civil Rights, & U.S. Department of Justice, Civil Rights Division, 2015); communicating in the parents' language builds trust and helps the parents to feel more comfortable attending events at the school. Not to mention that if the families can't read the invitation, they're not exactly likely to be able to attend. Please keep this advice in mind for pertinent student information as well, such as permission slips, progress reports, conference forms, and report cards. If it's possible to have translators available for events and conferences, even better!

- *Sponsor parent activities.* Hosting adult ESL classes, parent book clubs, and literacy nights can help to ignite parent engagement and interest, extending the joy of language and literacy to your students' families.

- *Host cultural events at the school.* These can include culture-specific holiday celebrations or "The World's Table"—a potluck for which students and parents can cook and bring traditional dishes from their cultures to offer. A Multicultural Night can be an incredibly joyous event where various cultures are celebrated with food, music, dance, and art that is representative of the school community. At a recent event, we saw the father of one of our students truly shine when he excitedly brought his entire mariachi band to perform. The joy was tremendous, and a spontaneous dance floor took shape!

- *Plan and host a community fair.* This type of event is often very popular in school districts. Contact local organizations, including parent/teacher associations; the fire and police departments; the local library, state, and county park organizations; and everything in between. Arrange for each group to have a table, and be prepared to share information about the resources available to local families with which they may not be familiar. Ask local businesses to donate items or gift certificates, assemble baskets to raffle off to families (for free!), and provide food and music to help boost attendance and create an all-around positive and joyous atmosphere. Families will appreciate the opportunity to learn about available community resources to which they are entitled and will enjoy an evening socializing together at the school, strengthening the home–school connection. This type of event also sends a strong message to families that the school values them and is dedicated to creating and maintaining a strong resource network built to suit their specific needs.

Lit 💡 Idea

Many times parents are unsure how they can work with their children at home, and multilingual parents are no exception. Hosting a Bilingual Family Literacy Night is a great way to introduce parents to literacy activities. Set up the library (or any space that works for the size of your population) into several centers with tables and chairs. Teachers can teach a mini-lesson to groups of parents and their children, including an interactive read-aloud, before introducing a hands-on activity. Then, parents can independently replicate the interactive read-aloud with their children before completing the activity, while the teachers are present to answer questions or otherwise assist as needed. This helps parents gain confidence in their ability to work with their children, bringing the joy of reading and literacy conversations home. End the evening by allowing families to shop for free books for readers of *all* ages in multiple languages, increasing the amount of literature available to both children and their older family members at home.

What's the Word? Vocabulary!

There are so many important facets of literacy instruction for MLLs, and it would be impossible to do them justice in one chapter. However, vocabulary has been identified as one of the main pillars, or foundational structures, of all literacy learning (and we mention it a lot in this book because, well, it's huge!). For these learners, vocabulary is unmistakably crucial in developing a strong foundation for language learning. In fact, "a rich vocabulary supports learning about the world, encountering new ideas, enjoying the beauty of language" (Beck et al., 2013, p. 1). In terms of our educational constructs, it is imperative to make vocabulary an intentional component of daily instruction. This means more than using the antiquated approach of giving students words and their definitions, then following up with an assessment after students have only a short exposure to and no true interaction with these words. A principal reason that students will not actually learn and use this new vocabulary, frankly, is because of the lack of interest. There is no authentic student engagement when new vocabulary is delivered in this manner. "Indeed, asking students to look up words in the dictionary and use them in a sentence is a stereotypical example of what students find uninteresting in school. . . . Among what needs to occur is that students keep using new words so they come to 'own' the words" (Beck et al., 2013, p. 14).

There are many avenues for students to obtain new vocabulary. Context is one method. Wide and voluminous reading allows students to encounter new vocabulary and to use context clues to work through their meaning. Block and Mangieri (2006) state that, "one way to increase students' vocabulary is to increase the amount of time they spend reading" (p. 21). There is no denying that frequent reading is an invaluable way to expose children to rich, new vocabulary. Through reading, students not only expand their vocabulary, but they are also able to practice and perfect pivotal literacy skills, which help in deciphering the meaning of new words. For example, students must use skills like identifying and using context clues, as well as decoding words, to assist them in vocabulary comprehension. For all learners, but especially MLLs, learning new words in context not only results in acquiring new English words, but it also presents students with the orthography of new words. "When learners encounter new language *in context,* they are afforded a range of contextual elements that support deeper connections between form (language) and meaning" (Giroir, Grimaldo, Vaughn, & Roberts, 2015, p. 640). Reading fluency and comprehension are facilitated by wide reading and a deeper vocabulary. "As our vocabulary increases, so does our ability to comprehend what we read. Likewise, as our comprehension skills increase, so does our ability to learn new words from context" (Block & Mangieri, 2006, p. 20). It is beneficial for the teacher to provide students with examples of how to use context clues in distinguishing the meaning of a word.

However capable the reader is in gleaning the meaning of new vocabulary words, research has proven that explicit vocabulary instruction is not only important, but vital in developing better readers and writers. Therefore, teachers ought to implement explicit vocabulary instruction in their daily lessons. Once again, it should be reiterated, vocabulary instruction should be more than doling out words and their definitions. For students to truly learn new words and build their repertoire, vocabulary instruction needs to be robust: "A robust approach to vocabulary involves diretly explaining the meaning of words along with thought-provoking, playful, and interactive follow-up" (Beck, McKeown, & Kucan, 2013, p. 3). Referring back to incorporating vocabulary instruction through context clues, Block and Mangieri (2006) equip teachers with well-established examples for teaching vocabulary through this method. They discuss providing examples of challenging words in context, and then using the following vocabulary activities: using context clues, the Vocabulary Self-Selection Strategy, and the Vocabulary Cloze Procedure (pp. 22–28). These vocabulary activities that teach new words can be implemented in all content-area classrooms.

Using context clues is certainly one way to begin worthwhile vocabulary instruction, but it should not be the only way. One "issue about relying on contexts is that many natural contexts are not all that informative for deriving word meaning" (Beck et al., 2013, p. 5). Therefore, other methodologies are necessary. Another way to teach new vocabulary is through word-building activities. In one type of activity, the teacher gives students a word and asks if they can make other words using only the letters found in the teacher-given word. "When the activity is over, and students have listed on the board some of the words they have made, you elaborate on the words, circling words in the same word families, talking about multiple meanings, pointing out spelling and meaning patterns, and discussing other words that may be related to the one that were made" (Block & Mangieri, 2006, p. 36). Another classroom word-building activity is to have students make and write words. In this activity, the teacher calls out different letters and manipulates sounds so that students can build new and different words. Students enjoy this type of activity because they are able to see the words transform (Block & Mangieri, 2006). In addition to being a fun and engaging activity, it allows students to manipulate letters and words and to see how many words they actually know. This activity utilizes the guidance of the teacher, "who provides clues and enough support so that even struggling students can be successful" (Block & Mangieri, 2006, p. 40).

One more vocabulary activity that can help foster vocabulary development for MLLs is word sorts, in which words can be sorted into different categories according to concepts or meaning. This is particularly useful for MLLs because they can sort pictures, instead of words, and arrange them in specific categories. For example,

A vocabulary graphic organizer is used to assist learners.

"without knowing the English term, they can sort pictures of a dog, a cat, a duck, and so on into an animal category. . . . English vocabulary is expanded as students repeat the sort, naming each picture and category with help from a teacher or peer" (Bear, Invernizzi, Templeton, & Johnston, 2008, p. 58). Once again, this is an activity that is not strictly confined to the ELA classroom. In fact, word sorts would be beneficial in a science or social studies classroom, as they can assist in building background knowledge or assessing background knowledge for a unit of study.

Assessing vocabulary can be a difficult task, which helps us to understand why teachers want to default to the timeless classic: end-of-the-week word and definition quiz! However, when it comes time to assess vocabulary, teachers need to decide what data they are trying to collect; what are they truly trying to assess? For example, does the teacher want to know if a student can use the word in a sentence, or if the student knows the definition, or if the student knows the appropriate context in which to use the word, or perhaps if the student knows associated words—like synonyms and antonyms. These considerations are important in determining the best assessment for your students. In their book, Block and Mangieri highlight both formal and informal tools for assessment. The formal assessments are a list of standardized tests that can be useful in assessing vocabulary retention. The informal assessments consist of different types that teachers can employ in their instruction. Some of the assessment formats they suggest are contextual, application definitional, contextual and definitional combined, morphological, rational/categorical, and analogy (Block & Mangieri, 2006, pp. 178–186). In another intriguing article, Stahl and Bravo (2010) propose an interesting assessment format called the Vocabulary Recognition Task. This type of assessment is fascinating because it presents a list of vocabulary and asks students to, basically, self-report on which ones they know. "The purpose was to identify content-related words that the students could both read and associate with a unit of study. . . . Its simplicity also makes it a user-friendly format for ELLs" (Stahl & Bravo, 2010, p. 571). Once again, it's important to identify what the teacher truly wants to know about a student's vocabulary retention, in order to implement the correct type of assessment. It seems to us that if we hear our students using the words we have taught in daily speech, or if we see them in their writing, it should be clear that students have adopted the word as their own.

Support the Educators

If you are new to teaching MLLs or are simply always interested in improving your language instruction, there are many great (free) resources available for educators. Twitter is a great place to start, with popular hashtags such as #ELLchat, #ESL, #WIDA, #TESOL, #SIOP, and #ELD. The authors are huge advocates of building a professional learning network (#PLN) on Twitter, and you can find us there regularly. Additionally, we offer a brief list of some of the most popular websites for those who work with MLLs. A word to the wise: This listing is just the tip of the iceberg. There are so many wonderful resources available online, and once you start looking for them, it may be difficult to pull yourself away. With that said, happy browsing!

- **Colorín Colorado**—This website is specifically designed for second-language and bilingual instruction. It provides educators, as well as parents, with resources, articles, and videos (*www.colorincolorado.org*).
- **Reading Rockets**—This website is focused predominantly on literacy and reading instruction, including a plethora of resources and articles for ELL instruction (*www.readingrockets.org*).
- **WIDA**—The WIDA website provides a wealth of information for the instruction of ELLs. The WIDA Consortium, made up of 40 states, territories, and federal agencies, is an authority in the field. It provides standards for teaching and learning, Can Do Descriptors to help teachers and students understand what to expect at various stages of English language development, and a wide variety of valuable resources (*https://wida.wisc.edu*).
- **RITELL Language and Country Projects**— This website, developed by the Rhode Island Teachers of English Language Learners, is a must for any teacher who has a student from another country on her roster. Here you will find presentations for various languages, created by graduate students and organized by world region and country, which provide an incredible amount of pertinent information from cultural norms to typical difficulties students may experience while learning English (*www.ritell.org/Language-and-Country-Projects*).
- **Tonya Ward Singer**—Singer's website is a fabulous resource providing free materials to help you better understand your MLLs, while also offering tools for instruction and assessment in language learning (*https://tonyasinger.com*).
- **Center for Applied Linguistics (CAL)**—The CAL website is particularly helpful for school and district administrators. This organization works to consistently provide valid and current research and best practices in the area of language acquisition, and it provides numerous resources from policy briefs to online professional development that can help you to guide your program in the right direction (*http://www.cal.org*).
- **CAL Sheltered Instruction Observation Protocol (SIOP)**—Even if your district has not implemented the SIOP model of working with MLLs, there is a great deal of useful information on this website, including lesson plans, free resources, and links to purchase SIOP products (*www.cal.org/siop/resources*).

Additionally, there are excellent research-based programs available to help guide your professional learning and development. The aforementioned SIOP model has been widely implemented by school districts through the series of texts written by Jana Echevarria, Maryellen Vogt, and Deborah Short and accompanying professional development. This model is especially effective when a sheltered instruction model for multilingual learner instruction is adopted in a district, and those MLLs spend the majority of their day in content-area classes with their English-speaking peers and teachers who are not certified to teach ESL. Of course, those students still receive support and instruction from certified ESL teachers, but it is necessary for the content-area teachers to be familiar and comfortable with the strategies and best practices that work for MLLs. If you're a school or district administrator, and you're not sure where to start, researching the SIOP model may be well worth your time.

CONCLUSION

MLLs are becoming more common in our classrooms, yet teachers are often under-prepared to work with them effectively. As leaders in literacy, we need to advocate for best practices to be provided to our multilingual students and their families, whether that means revamping classroom libraries, accommodating students' needs with varied and differentiated activities, or, importantly, helping teachers to refresh and shift their mindsets to create a community that is welcoming to all and celebrates multilingualism and multiculturalism. This is not easy work, but it is vitally important work, and you will be leading the charge! When you approach this population with authentic positivity, genuine interest, and cultural awareness, you will create a bridge for these families connecting a celebration of their languages and cultures with the joy of learning and literacy.

Lit 💡 Idea

If you are an administrator or teacher-leader, secure permission to host focus groups to interview students and get feedback regarding the existing curriculum and program areas of study. Ask the students: How supported do you feel by your teachers? How are our programs working?

Stop, Think, and Take Action

Based on the ideas presented in this chapter on engaging and joyful advocacy for working with MLLs, take time to consider the ways in which you might get everyone involved to support readers and writers in your local school community. Reflect on the following:

If your role is that of a . . .

- **Classroom teacher** or **teacher-leader**—Ask yourself, "How can I make sure my MLLs are comfortable learning in my class? How can I collaborate with the ESL or bilingual teacher to ensure best practices and acquire worthwhile assessments for language growth?"

- **Literacy specialist** or **literacy coach**—Ask yourself, "How might I work closely with ESL teachers to weld MLL and literacy strategies? What new and old literacy strategies can be shared with the ESL teachers and classroom teachers to better assist language learning?"

- **School administrator** or **school-level leader**—Ask yourself, "What supports are necessary for bridging the gap between school and home for MLLs [e.g., providing interpreters for parent–teacher conferences and CST meetings or translating school documents in languages other than English]?"

- **District administrator** or **district-level leader**—Ask yourself, "How can I support teachers and building leaders in celebrating culture at the school level, or at the district level?" Commit to a district vision that focuses on providing students with windows, mirrors, and sliding glass doors through the texts available throughout your schools, and ensure that it is appropriately funded.

- **Professional developer**—Ask yourself, **"**Do I know enough about effective best practices for MLLs to introduce the work to my teachers? If not, how can I become more competent in this area in order to support both teachers and children on their journey to competency? What professional development can I seek out to attend and make available to staff?"

CHAPTER 9

Family Literacy

It is the school's responsibility to figure out how
to welcome parents into the educational process.
—PATRICIA A. EDWARDS

Mrs. Calabrese has been notified by Mrs. Diskin that additional federal funds have been
made available to support the needs of immigrant students and their families. Although the
amount is much less than expected, Mrs. Calabrese believes that no amount is too small if
it puts books in the hands of kids and engages families in joyful ways. She meets with Mrs.
Griffin and Mrs. Rosenfeld to discuss how to spend the money, and the team comes up with
a playful name for a series of six after-school family events. "Bienvenidos Book Club, it is!"
exclaims Mrs. Griffin. Overhearing the excitement from the main office, Mrs. DeMarco walks
in and announces that she wants to be part of the planning committee. The team decides to
brainstorm a list of six themes aligned with the unique experiences that immigrant students
and their families face when attending school in a new country. Already, a list of children's
books and authors is suggested by the reading specialist, Mrs. Rosenfeld.

STUDENTS' RIGHTS TO INTEGRATED SUPPORT SYSTEMS

We've all heard of the phrase "it takes a village to raise a child," but even more so, it
takes an integrated approach wherein everyone is working together for the common
good of a child. In Chapter 4, one aspect of that complex system of stakeholders was
introduced, as we discussed the knowledge-building framework that exists when professional learning and professional development are a focus. But what about families
and caregivers, volunteers, and community members? According to Dwyer, Kunz,
and Simpson (2019), "Learning occurs as a result of overlapping, multifaceted spheres
of influence, and when this complexity of education systems is recognized, there
is a stronger likelihood that all stakeholders will work as partners toward the same,

collective goal" (p. 2). Let's unpack how we can work together to forge a strong connection with our families and communities.

FAMILY LITERACY

The Scholastic (2019a) *Kids and Family Reading Report* recognizes that the top predictors of reading frequency include (1) a feeling that reading is fun, (2) a viewpoint that reading is important, and (3) having parents who are readers. This is why many organizations such as Reach Out and Read are working with hospitals and pediatricians across the country to get books in the hands of parents from the very start. As literacy changemakers, we can get involved with similar organizations to promote early literacy and access to books directly in our local school communities. In one instance, one of our colleagues noticed that over the summer there were lots of parents waiting outside of the central offices to register their children for school. While many of the students were preparing to enter kindergarten that school year, they often arrived with their younger siblings and a gathering of relatives and caretakers. So, this administrator created a book bin of sorts with crayons and writing materials to place in the waiting area, with a sign stating that families could take a book home. Full disclaimer: Not everyone in the district was as enlightened as this literacy leader, and on a few occasions the book bin either (1) went missing or (2) was returned to the curriculum area as a microaggression. Nonetheless, she persisted! When family literacy is concerned, we need to reach out and engage in joyful ways, and focus our efforts on promoting reading habits and getting books in the households of the students we serve. When planning for family literacy events, we have all experienced the naysayer who discredits that anyone will attend the event or does not appreciate the efforts made to plan one: we say push forward with your integrated supports, think big, plan for joy, and the rest will fall into place.

First Impressions Matter

Edwards (2009) reminds us of the importance of creating a positive environment for families that includes (1) welcoming signs and banners, (2) attractive bulletin board spaces, (3) welcoming letters, (4) newsletters, and (5) surveys. We agree that these five elements should be at the heart of every school community's outreach in engaging parents, and have witnessed great things happening when these elements are always present, and promote student learning and joy. Intermediate Principal Erin Embon takes this process a step further by including a monthly "Parent Advisory" at her school. Here, parents have an opportunity to share information about their child's strengths and needs, while updating the school faculty and leadership about upcoming events in the community. In many instances, parents are invited to share their visions for their children's education, for their children as students, and for their children's future (Edwards, 2009). Prior to launching schoolwide literacy initiatives, Mrs. Embon utilizes a space set up specifically for parent–teacher collaboration to get feedback about topics like intervention and support for readers and writers, summer reading initiatives, the transition from elementary to middle school and from middle school to high school, and updates to the language arts curriculum and program. At one event, in response to parents who were overwhelmingly in support of advocating for a stronger intervention system, the supervisor of instruction recommended creating a position for a literacy specialist. Due to support from the local community and the administration's effort to secure funding, the position was created, and a literacy specialist was hired to provide interventions for the following school year. Edwards (2009) states, "The parent focus group meeting is an opportunity for parents to voice their opinions on a variety of issues. It's a public forum. Parents can talk about what's on their minds" (p. 39). When focusing on literacy, we recommend using the structure in Figure 9.1 to facilitate a 1-hour meeting. Of course, this schedule can be adjusted based on time and need.

Every Student Is Someone's Child: Moving beyond Levels and Deficits

In all of our interactions with families and parents, we must keep in mind that the literacy development of students is complex, and, while knowing a child's reading level is helpful information for the classroom teacher, parents need to be engaged in discussions about their child's specific strengths and areas of needed improvement. More helpful than telling a parent "Your child is a level M," would be an explanation such as "I notice that your child loves graphic novels. I've created a list of progressions here for you, showing how we might keep him engaged as he works his way through these amazing series. A strength is that your child has excellent decoding skills and always seems to read with fluency and expression. I'm proud of how he is reading in longer and more meaningful phrases. However, sometimes he has a difficult time recalling information from the text. We've recently been working on a strategy called 'stop and jot' to get him to reflect after reading about a palmful of information in the texts. This would be a great strategy to reinforce at home. Tell me, what are some reading behaviors you've noticed, if any?" As you can see, there's a stark difference between

---

10 minutes—Welcome and introductions.

5 minutes—What have you been reading lately? (Share a few "must reads" and contemporary titles with optional giveaways.)

20 minutes—Literacy best-practices discussion: Highlight a few key ideas related to your school's literacy curriculum or program. Engage the parents in a brief presentation of what you hope to accomplish.

20 minutes—Allow time for Q&A. Have materials on hand to collect parents' ideas and responses (e.g., chart paper, index cards, markers). Have a recorder jot down notes from the discussion.

5 minutes—Wrap-up and next steps.

FIGURE 9.1. A sample agenda for organizing a family literacy parent-advisory or focus group.

the binary approach to considering a child either (1) proficient or (2) not proficient, versus providing detailed information about observed passions for reading, interests, strengths, and targeted areas of needed improvement. The students we serve are the children of very caring families with networks of support. Our mantra is: they are the reason we are here.

Lit Idea

When reaching out to the home for the first time, always begin with something positive that you have observed about the child. Consider making it a reading interest! Imagine calling home with a fun anecdote about a book that you collaboratively enjoyed with the student: "Your child and I had the best time almost falling out of our seats over the latest book in *The Adventures of Captain Underpants* series. Tell me, how is this school year going for your child?"

Programs for Parents and Families: Step into Bienvenidos Book Club

In addition to prioritizing family literacy and making first impressions count, we have to also intentionally design opportunities for parents and families to get involved. In Chapter 8 you read about the ways in which we can get involved to support our multilingual learners. In this chapter, we offer a glimpse into "Bienvenidos Book Club," a family literacy program with features aimed at engaging the families of immigrant students (see Figure 9.2).

When the program first began, our literacy colleagues looked into the number of languages and countries represented in a small 4-mile-square radius of a school

Coming Soon...

Bienvenidos Book Club!

This program is for students in grades Kindergarten-3rd Grade and their parents/guardians/families.

- Receive free books
- Enjoy refreshments
- Spend time together learning and enjoying reading and writing
- Celebrate language and culture

The six sessions will begin on Monday, April 8th. Sessions will be held in the evening from 5:30 to 7:00p.m. at Parker School.

Let us know if you are interested in joining us!

Yes, I am interested in attending the "Bienvenidos Book Club!"

Child's Name________
Grade________
School: ________
Teacher ________
Adult's Name________
Phone Number________

Próximamente...

Bienvenidos Book Club!

Este programa es para estudiantes en los grados Kinder-3 grado y sus padres / tutores / familias.

- Recibir libros gratis
- Disfruta de refrescos
- Pasen tiempo juntos aprendiendo y disfrutando de la lectura y la escritura
- Celebrar el lenguaje y la cultura

Las seis sesiones comenzarán el lunes 8 de abril. Las sesiones serán de ayuda por la tarde de 5:30 a 7:00 p.m. en la escuela Parker.

Háganos saber si está interesado en unirse a nosotros!

Si, estoy interesado en asistir al "Bienvenidos Book Club!"

Nombre del niño________
Grado________
Esquela ________
Profesor ________
Nombre del adulto________
Número de teléfono________

FIGURE 9.2. A sample set of invitations sent home to parents in multiple languages.

community in central New Jersey. We were surprised to find out that in this small community, 25 countries and 17 spoken languages were represented among immigrant families (with Spanish topping the list). Immediately, we used federal funds from Title III—Language Instruction for English Learners and Immigrant Students to begin planning the Bienvenidos Book Club. Remember, no amount of funding is too little. Get to know the cultures in your school community and design literacy experiences that will benefit your students and their families. In Figure 9.3, we share a sample graphic organizer for collecting information about students' countries of origin; general values, beliefs, and practices; home life and interaction, and how children and school are viewed. Gathering this information is just one way to get a baseline for what can be done to engage families. Recall that in Chapter 8 we provided a reference to the RITELL Language and Country Projects, which can help you supplement the information needed to gain a comprehensive understanding of the families you serve.

For example, in the Bienvenidos Book Club, collecting data resulted in the formation of a 6-week-long club for immigrant students and their families. The name "Bienvenidos" was chosen to symbolize a welcome to our literacy community. Each evening included three children's books that were intentionally selected to serve as mirrors for the participating readers. These three books were aligned with a theme for each evening, beginning with the importance of names. Students who participated

Materials are organized for another evening of the "Bienvenidos Book Club," with books readily available for attendees to take home.

THE CULTURES IN MY COMMUNITY				
Country of origin	General values, beliefs, and practices	Home life and interaction	How children are viewed	How school is viewed

FIGURE 9.3. A graphic organizer for collecting information about the cultures in your school community.

in all six sessions received a total of 18 children's books to add to their home libraries. In addition, we had opportunities to Skype with authors like Emma Otheguy. Of course, the pizza and snacks also added a nice touch to the family literacy engagement evening. If you offer it, they will come!

> ## Lit 💡 Idea
>
> As you get to know the students and the families in your school community, design a unique book club experience based on your students' backgrounds, cultures, and interests. Utilize your school librarian or local literacy experts to design a set of themes with books and accompanying activities.

A Summer Reading Initiative

Nestled in the heart of Middlesex County, New Jersey, is a charming K–2 school led by Dr. Remi Christofferson, a proud and passionate principal with a penchant for literacy teaching and learning. Working with the district administration, Dr. Christofferson decided to set aside Title 1 federal funds for students to self-select books for summer reading, while adding to their home libraries. We all know that the summer slide and loss of traction with reading during these months can be traced back to long gaps from instruction combined with limited access to books and literacy experiences at home. Follow these steps that this school's literacy changemakers took to remediate that problem:

- *Step 1.* Determine how much funding you have available and identify the students who are in need of literacy support materials (e.g., high-quality books).
- *Step 2.* Work with a local book vendor to get access to catalogues or other resources that the students can shop from.
- *Step 3.* Engage the literacy team at your school in helping students "spend-down" their money as they choose books.
- *Step 4.* Order the books along with "book baggies" and wait for delivery (following purchase-order procedures and protocols).
- *Step 5.* Orchestrate the help of the literacy team when the books arrive. Sort the books based on students' individualized orders. Half of the books go in the "book baggies," and the other half of the books are set aside and labeled with the students' names and home addresses.
- *Step 6.* Allow students to take half of the books home on the last day of school. Students leave excited with their book baggies.
- *Step 7.* Mail the remaining half of the books to the students' homes over the summer, reminding students and their families about the joy and importance of reading (especially over the summer!).

If you believe that these steps seem tedious or sound like a lot of work, let this anecdote sink in. After shopping for books, a small child catches a glimpse of a familiar

Literacy leaders prepare to mail books to students on a summer afternoon.

administrator in the school hallway. He shouts, "Thank you so much for letting me shop for my own books!" The rest is joy.

CONCLUSION

A core element of literacy and joy is an integrated support system that intentionally works to serve the best interests of readers and writers. This work involves literacy changemakers, who first recognize the importance of getting parents and families on board. It involves getting books in the hands of our kids and tailoring programs to meet the unique needs of the diverse school communities where our students live. Create a welcoming environment, be open to hearing and addressing any challenges faced by families in your community through open forums, solicit help from parents as needed, and let no one get in the way of your team, as you unstoppably get parents more involved and work on behalf of all readers and writers (Edwards, 2009).

Family Literacy Nights

Mrs. Schiano, a literacy coach at Hatchery Hill, has coordinated several very well attended family literacy nights. When asked for her advice, she responded that she has a terrific and helpful team, and that they work hard before the event to make sure that children and their parents will be there. First she and her team, along with help from their students, decide on the theme of the evening. Some examples include Family

Picnic, Read in Your Pajamas, and Winter Wonderland. They next write letters and make personal visits to the local businesses to ask for donations to help fund (and feed!) the literacy nights. The donations they acquire go into baskets that are raffled off on these special evenings.

Now it's time to make the school community aware of the event. Letters in several languages go home to parents, and children meet to plan and design decor. The "frenzy" builds over the next few weeks, since students know that they will get to show off to their families, eat pizza or some other local dish, and, ultimately, take home free books.

Once children and their parents arrive at the school, they are greeted by student hosts and shown to the cafeteria, where a meal awaits them. Music is playing, and they are impressed by the student-made decor. Everyone is already in a great mood! After having eaten, children and their parents circulate among five or six rooms (literacy stations) in which they might buddy read, take a fluency walk, present a readers' theatre play, play a vocabulary game, or write a poem. Teachers are in each room, ready to welcome families.

An engaging literacy station with props is prepared in advance of a Family Literacy Night.

At the end of the evening, the baskets are raffled off, and each child is allowed to choose books to take home. These events have gone a long way toward making school feel less intimidating to parents and homier for our children. Take a chance—invite families to join you for an evening of literacy fun!

Stop, Think, and Take Action

Based on the ideas presented in this chapter on family literacy, take time to consider the ways in which you might take action to tap the potential of parents, families, and the local school community. Reflect on the following:

If your role is that of a . . .

- **Classroom teacher** or **teacher-leader**—Start off small by collecting literacy stories from just a few of the families in your classroom. Utilize survey tools to learn about the students' strengths and areas of needed improvement in addition to the parents' visions for each child.

- **Literacy specialist** or **literacy coach**—Work with your district administration and literacy changemakers to drum up support for a family literacy night. Look back at the chapter for ideas about how you can tailor the event to meet the needs of students in your school community.

- **School administrator** or **school-level leader**—Collect information about how many origin countries and languages are represented in your particular school. Design something special based on your findings.

- **District administrator** or **district-level leader**—Set aside funding that addresses family engagement and increasing the number of books in students' home collections. Work with other literacy changemakers who have experience utilizing federal, state, and local funding sources.

- **Professional developer**—Create a strong partnership with a book vendor in your state or region. Meet with your representative quarterly to learn about new high-quality children's books and materials that are available.

CHAPTER 10

New Literacies and Technology

As new literacies that include digital and media technologies evolve, preparing students to understand and adjust to these literacy demands is critical to current and future expectations for pleasure and work.
—DIANE BARONE AND TODD E. WRIGHT

Elevators didn't put stairs out of business.
—DONALYN MILLER

The literacy changemakers at Hatchery Hill recognize that students have a right to access books in both digital and print formats, but are against requiring extended screen time for students that has no purpose. Mrs. Griffin is excited about the one-to-one digital devices initiative that was rolled out at the beginning of the school year, but cautious about how the devices are being utilized. She calls a meeting with Mrs. Rosenfeld and Mrs. Calabrese to discuss the research related to the literacy needs of students and finding the right integration of digital instruction. Although some teachers are having students draft their writing on their computers, Mrs. DeMarco finds that the use of a traditional writing notebook for planning and drafting has resulted in better outcomes for learners. The team decides to create a plan for recalibrating literacy practices, and commits to developing a "Not This, But That" list for using digital technology in the classroom. Mrs. Diskin brings to the attention of the team that a significant amount of money is being spent on a subscription for an online tool that is rarely utilized at Hatchery Hill. Mrs. Schiano suggests alternative uses for this money, as some free apps and online tools are now available. Mrs. Griffin determines that canceling the subscription is the best option at this time, but reallocates the money to allow teachers to buy digital mentor texts.

NEW LITERACIES FOR OUR FUTURE

Despite some of the trepidations that are often involved with using digital and media technologies in the classroom, we know that understanding and adjusting to these literacy demands is critical for the expectations we have for pleasure and work both now and in the future (Barone & Wright, 2008). Effectively using the Internet, engaging with one-to-one technologies, accessing web-based resources for reading and writing, utilizing applications and software, and communicating through a journey of ever-evolving new literacies are just a few of many expectations that society and the workforce have for our students. These expectations require that teachers have a positive attitude about the use of technology and not get involved in a "technology for the sake of technology" manner of implementation. All too often, we see school districts purchase districtwide subscriptions to digital tools and programs that support compliance over creative innovation in our instructional design.

Does a class deserve an award for the most hours logged in a digital-reading application program, or do we seek examples of transformative ways in which students' abilities to read, write, listen, speak, and view are further developed? Asking these questions is especially important when considering our earliest readers. Some of the most prevalent statements about our early readers and the use of digital resources are that (1) high-quality media should support content and curricular goals with few distractors; (2) integration of digital technology should enhance learning along with other materials and activities; (3) the use of technology should support creativity, exploration, collaboration, problem solving, and knowledge development; (4) technology can strengthen home–school connections; and (5) access to assistive technologies can support equitable literacy learning outcomes (Paciga, O'Brien, Kucirkova, & O'Clair, 2019). In essence these digital resources need to support the development of even our earliest readers and writers, and must serve a greater purpose than keeping students occupied and rewarded for screen time.

In her bestselling book *The Happiness Project: Or Why I Spent a Year Trying to Sing in the Morning, Clean My Closets, Fight Right, Read Aristotle, and Generally Have More Fun,* Rubin (2015) also warns that if we reward people for doing an activity, they will often believe that it's "work" and not something that can be done for fun. Similar to our belief that reading logs are a fictitious romance and false reality, we should not tell ourselves that school- and districtwide compliance with using digital programs to log "screen time" will result in proficient and more joyful learners. There is no silver bullet. Rather, we offer a number of alternatives in this chapter that paint a picture of new literacies and technologies that can be used in imaginative, productive, and joyful ways.

GETTING DIGITAL WITH MENTOR TEXTS

Students have the right to access reading materials in both print and digital formats (International Literacy Association, 2018a). However, our coaching experiences have collectively led us to believe that there are often times when high-quality children's books and mentor texts are dismissed by students as "too babyish" or "too childish," especially when these print formats are shared with students in the upper grades. A simple solution to this phenomenon is to get digital with mentor texts, because daily read-alouds are important across all grade levels. The "book whisperer," Donalyn Miller, reminds us that if being read aloud to is only considered an early childhood or elementary need, one might begin to question why so many adults are attracted to digital read-aloud formats like podcasts and Audible.

There are many benefits to using digital mentor texts. First, all students are able to access the text and print features (e.g. illustrations, captions, photographs) because the digital text is displayed in a whole-class area. This facilitates a shared reading experience and can help to engage the students in text-dependent questioning related to the material. According to Fisher and Frey (2015), the four main focus areas for asking text-dependent questions are:

1. What does the text *say*? (literally)
2. How does the text *work*?
3. What does the text *mean*?
4. What does the text *inspire you to do*?

While having a print copy of the text allows for the teacher to demonstrate concepts of print and allows students to later go back and engage with a physical copy of the reading material, a digital display allows for interactive annotating, text discussions, and a shared reading experience. An added bonus is that readers have increased access to books for some spur-of-the-moment read-aloud opportunities. As readers and literacy changemakers, many of us share in the satisfaction of immediately heading to the local library or bookstore to grab a copy of a compelling read. Fast shipping and online services have increased the speed at which print copies of reading materials are delivered. We are no doubt guilty of this "Amazon-esia" effect, whereby books arrive at speeds that make it difficult to even remember what was ordered. However, there are also times when we need to seize the joy and need access to books right away. Consider the following scenarios:

- *Classroom teacher*—The students have expressed their interest in learning more about animals that live in a local ecosystem. Immediately, the teacher seizes an opportunity to download a digital text to share after lunch and recess.
- *Literacy specialist*—There is one student who happens to be having an "off" day and could use a little pick-me-up. Knowing that he has an interest in a popular superhero, the teacher is able to adapt the lesson to include a mentor text to boost his spirits.
- *School administrator*—A substitute shortage has led to a circumstance in which an hour of your Friday afternoon will be spent covering a class in your building. You immediately log into your digital account to download a favorite childhood book to share with the students. What had seemed like a hassle has just turned into the best part of your day.
- *District administrator*—You have been invited to be a guest speaker at a district event and believe that an inspirational read-aloud would connect with the attendees. You download *What Do You Do with a Chance?* by Kobi Yamada (2018) and peruse the text to practice reading with fluency and expression.
- *Professional developer*—As a reading coach, the seventh-grade team informs you that they need your help in launching a unit on dystopian fiction. You can

A partial look at a K–12 literacy consultant's Kindle Cloud Reader collection.

picture some perfect selections sitting on your bookshelf at home, but you need to take the opportunity now to start planning. Luckily, you find some digital resources to help you and the teachers get to work.

Even though Chapter 5 in this book highlights the key ingredients that contribute to dynamic learning environments—including classroom libraries and print materials that are interdisciplinary, inclusive, and diverse—one can appreciate the versatile benefits of utilizing digital formats as well.

A Deeper Dive into Diverse Formats

Utilizing the K–12 series of *Your Literacy Standards Companion* texts (Blauman & Burke, 2017; Burke, 2017a, 2017b; Taberski & Burke, 2017), Dr. Ken Kunz and teacher Brian Benavides drafted some sample lessons (see Figures 10.1–10.3) in order to demonstrate how diverse media formats, including digital mentor-text videos, illustrations, paintings, and maps can be used to engage readers across K–12 contexts. Using Reading Anchor Standard 7 from the New Jersey Department of Education (2019), they identified the gist of the literacy standard for each grade span and sought ways to enhance the essence of student learning through new literacies.

PROMOTING COLLABORATION THROUGH TECHNOLOGY TOOLS

In addition to having on-demand access to digital resources and mentor texts, many literacy leaders aim to promote communication and collaboration through the use of technology tools. In essence, technology can work wonders when our goal is to get students talking about what they are reading. These tools can also be used to build a reading community that has a shared sense of urgency regarding the importance

READING ANCHOR STANDARD 7
SAMPLE K–5 LESSON

- **Gist: Integrate and evaluate content presented in diverse media and formats.**
- **Focus Question:** How does this media format differ from what other forms of media say about the same subject? What is the "subject"?
- **Objective:** Students will analyze an interpretation of two media videos, identifying the subject and creating a list of questions.

Lesson Progression

Day 1	Day 2	Day 3	Day 4
Zooming In on Illustrations	**Text Activity**	**Clarifying Images**	**Putting It All Together**
Strategy: Zoom in on two different illustrations in *Standing Up to Bullies* to gain more information about the characters, setting, and plot.	The teacher reads aloud *Strictly No Elephants* by Lisa Mantchev and Taeeun Yoo **Strategy:** Questioning the Text	**Strategy:** Seek to clarify! How do the images in the Disney Pixar video *Lou* make the topic clear?	**Strategy:** Complete a three-column chart in small groups to take notes about each media format. Why is it helpful as a reader to collectively gain information from illustrations, images, and texts?

Resources:
- **Illustrations:** From Reading A–Z (*www.readinga-z.com*) *Standing Up to Bullies*
- **Digital Mentor Text:** *Strictly No Elephants* by Lisa Mantchev and Taeeun Yoo
- **Video:** *www.pixar.com/lou*

Vocabulary Word Wall

print
digital
information
content

Three-Column Chart

Text 1: *Standing Up to Bullies*	*Strictly No Elephants*	Video: Disney Pixar's *Lou*

FIGURE 10.1. A sample K–5 lesson utilizing diverse formats.

READING ANCHOR STANDARD 7
SAMPLE 6–8 LESSON

- **Gist:** Integrate and evaluate content presented in diverse media and formats, including by visual and quantitative means, as well as in words.
- **Focus Question:** What is the topic/subject of the written text? How does the oral format (recording or performance) help me understand?
- **Objective:** Students will analyze diverse media formats through the lens of social justice and equity for LGBTQIA individuals.

Lesson Progression

Day 1	Day 2	Day 3	Day 4
Mentor Text Activity	**Video Interpretation**	**Photograph Activity**	**Research**
Strategy:	**Strategy:**	**Strategy:**	Based on our recent work, what is the topic, question, or problem that you still have questions about?
How do the pictures and captions in the text help you to better understand the main idea?	Listen to the video. Notice and explain how this visual information helps you better understand the read-aloud from our previous lesson.	Complete a Venn diagram in small groups to take notes about each media format.	Read! Research! Reach out to an expert!

Resources:
- **Digital Mentor Text:** *The Stonewall Riots: Coming Out in the Streets* by Gayle E. Pitman
- **YouTube Video:** The Day the Stonewall Riots Shook America (*https://youtu.be/tCFwOJcMjMO*)
- **Photographs:** From Google Image searches for "Stonewall Riots"

Vocabulary Word Wall

digital text
diverse formats
visual information
integrate

Venn Diagram

The Stonewall Riots: Video: The Day the Stonewall Riots
Coming Out in the Streets   Shook America

FIGURE 10.2. A sample 6–8 lesson utilizing diverse formats.

READING ANCHOR STANDARD 7
SAMPLE 9–12 LESSON

- **Gist: Integrate and evaluate content presented in diverse media and formats.**
- **Focus Question:** How does this media format differ from what other forms of media say about the same subject? What is the "subject"?
- **Objective:** Students will analyze an interpretation of two media videos, identifying the subject and creating a list of questions.

Lesson Progression

Day 1	Day 2	Day 3	Day 4
The Tale of Two Videos	**Paired Text Activity**	**Painting Activity**	**Map Analysis**
Strategy: Generate a list of questions you still have after viewing the videos "Bachata En Kingston" and "Espuma y Arrecife."	*Celia Cruz: Queen of Salsa* by Veronica Chambers **Strategy:** List more questions and start to compare and contrast different ways in which the subjects are presented.	**Strategy:** Complete a three-column chart in small groups to take notes about each media format.	In the first video we viewed, the video shows no beach at all, even though the data on the map show that most Afro-Colombians live along the coastline. Where do you think they are? Provide evidence from the video to support your ideas.

Resources:
- **YouTube Videos:** "Bachata En Kingston" (*https://youtu.be/_AHNTdSfa40*) and "Espuma y Arrecife" (*https://youtu.be/stQOxae350Y*)
- **Digital Mentor Text:** *Celia Cruz: Queen of Salsa* by Veronica Chambers
- **Painting Examples**
- **Map:** Population Map of the African Colombian population in Colombia

Vocabulary Word Wall

interpretation
diverse formats
artistic mediums
representation of a subject

Three-Column Notes Chart

Video 1:	Video 2:	Painting:

FIGURE 10.3. A sample 9–12 lesson utilizing diverse formats.

of reading and collaborating respectfully with one another. Recognizing that there would be three literacy courses during the semester, with approximately 50 students across all of the sections, Dr. Ken Kunz decided to create a set of class pages using Flipgrid, a digital platform where students can record and share short videos. Three focus questions guided the online introduction:

1. Tell us your name and what it means to you.
2. Share an early literacy experience.
3. Explain any academic or personal goals that you have for this semester.

This experience enables the teacher to make connections between names and faces, while also learning the correct pronunciation of students' names, an effort that can have a great impact and shows that we value students' identities (McLaughlin, 2016). In addition, having students tell about a past experience and state their academic and social–emotional (personal) goals creates a stronger bond between the students and their teacher, while also enhancing bonds between the students themselves. Of course, there are educators who teach over 100 readers and writers in each marking period, making this tool that much more valuable. It is no wonder why many educators proudly announce that they have caught "Flipgrid Fever."

Lit 💡 Idea

Go to *www.flipgrid.com* and create a free account to get started. Think of two to three items of importance to you in getting to know (1) teachers in your school community or (2) readers and writers in your classroom. Create a space for recording and sharing. Later, view the videos to notice any trends or areas of joy that can expand the important literacy work ahead. Perhaps many of the participants find it difficult to name a favorite author or book from childhood. If that's the case, it's a perfect time to get teachers or students familiar with book talks and a plethora of amazing authors and texts!

Apps and Digital Tools That Work

By the time this book is resting in your hands, countless apps and tools for technology have likely grown by leaps and bounds. Therefore, we caution that this discussion on apps and tools that work simply highlights some of the resources that have brought us joy when working with readers and writers. As we reflect on experiences that have increased student motivation and engagement, we recognize that many tools that we rely on for support continue to evolve, and even become obsolete in some cases. Nonetheless, using technology and apps is a great way to increase student engagement and foster student-led activities. These 21st-century methods often replace some of the more traditional reader's response activities, including the mundane book report. We encourage you to think about letting go of these seemingly more "comfortable" reader's response activities, and we give you permission to remove them from your toolkits. Instead, add to your repertoire technology and apps that can support everyone from your striving readers who struggle with traditional reader's response activities to advanced students who seek new platforms for sharing ideas far and wide. Some benefits are:

- Students can engage in collaborative discourse.
- Writing skills can be utilized and enhanced through the use of new literacies.
- Students can exercise their oral expression abilities.

Podcasts

When we asked for contributions to our technology chapter, we knew that we could rely on the work of Gena Cooley (@theteachernme) and Elaine Mendez (@Elem-Coach). After all, their presentation at a local New Jersey EdCamp was on fire when they discussed using digital technology tools. Gena and Elaine assert that podcasts are a great way to allow students to share their views, opinions, and ideas through audio devices (see Figure 10.4). Students are able to take charge of the format, presentation, and their learning through this medium. Podcasts also allow teachers to do formative assessments of their students' understanding of various content that was previously taught.

Lit 💡 Idea

Visit *www.vocaroo.com* or *www.twistedwave.com* and access the free online resources. Students can digitally record themselves. The teacher can show students how to save their work and create QR codes that can be shared with parents or posted on an interactive bulletin board in the hallway or classroom environment.

Websites and Blogs

Websites and blogs are other mediums through which students can showcase their understanding and talents utilizing more visual methods (see Figure 10.5). Students

---

Students can . . .
- complete an author or character analysis,
- share a book review or book recommendation,
- compare and contrast different viewpoints or ideas presented in the text,
- conduct an interview and present the findings,
- lead a conference,
- retell a story,
- listen to a teacher recording the directions for an assignment that is required (during a child's absence from school), and/or
- make connections to the text.

FIGURE 10.4. Suggestions for utilizing podcasts in the literacy classroom.

Students can . . .
- create blog posts;
- write book reviews or engage in book talks and discussions;
- create mock interviews related to the characters in a text or interview school faculty, staff, and friends;
- write a digital story;
- begin a video diary;
- engage in virtual field trips; and/or
- design a virtual learning portfolio as a reader or writer.

FIGURE 10.5. Suggestions for utilizing websites and blogs in the literacy classroom.

can create videos, share virtual portfolios, and blog to create an ongoing journal of their ideas. Imagine giving students digital opportunities to highlight their lives in books or their lives as writers! These options provide a great way to show their learning growth and progression throughout the school year.

What's Popular Right Now?

When getting started with this chapter, we put out a call to our professional learning community on Twitter for technology "shoutouts." The resources in Figure 10.6 include digital tools that broaden our awareness of what exists to help students become more passionate, skillful, and motivated readers. This list helps to demonstrate the power of a literacy professional learning network. In just 24 hours, we found ourselves checking out some new tools, along with those that are tried and true and dear to our work with students. What tools are you using to promote joyful literacy classrooms?

CONCLUSION

In this chapter, we present a number of ideas for engaging with new literacies in the classroom. Now, we'd like to hear from you! Nothing is better than witnessing the joy that is experienced from using digital and media technologies, and we encourage you to use the hashtag #literacystrong on Twitter and Instagram. Tag us about some of the ways that new literacies are being utilized imaginatively in your classroom. Here's how to connect with us digitally:

Dr. Ken Kunz:
@DrKennethKunz (Twitter)
@FarviewLittleFreeLibrary (Instagram)

Dr. Rachel Lella:
@rlellaEdD (Twitter)
#literacystrong

An Incomplete List of Our Digital Favorites	
Resource	**How it promotes joy in the literacy classroom**
Flipgrid	Visit *www.flipgrid.com* (referenced in the chapter) and get started. Start with book talks or "Getting to Know the Reader" introductions!
#BookSnaps	Readers can use the hashtag on Twitter and social media to give enticing book talks, encouraging other students to read books that have spoken to their hearts.
Animoto	*Animoto.com* allows teachers (and students) to create free digital videos. We love using this resource to create digital book talks. Check out our sample book talk using *My Diary from Here to There* by Amada Irma Perez (*https://tinyurl.com/samplebooktalk*).
SeeSaw	Let your students upload their annotations to SeeSaw (*https://web.seesaw.me*). Students can comment on one another's digital annotations and explain their thinking. Try it with a grade-level complex text to increase student motivation and engagement!
Kahoot and Gimkit	If you like using Kahoot (*www.kahoot.com*) for formative assessment, you will also love the interactive features of Gimkit (*www.gimkit.com*). Students enjoy "powering up" as they earn money and buy advantages.
Learning Ally	This accommodating learning tool is an audiobook option for students with learning disabilities, visual impairments, or physical disabilities. Many dyslexia advocates have recommended this resource as well. *www.learningally.org*
Recommended by Our "Twitterverse" Professional Learning Network	
Google Slides	Part of Google Suite includes Google Slides, a tool for creating more interactive presentations. Students can embed videos, choose from many themes, and collaborate and share their learning with others. *www.google.com/slides/about*
Keynote	Apple has created a tool in which students can bring slides and presentations to life. *www.apple.com/keynote*
PicCollage and Canva	Allow time for your students to get visually creative with pictures! *https://piccollage.com* *www.canva.com*
BookCreator	Students can partner write to create interactive stories, or work on their own to bring their favorite drafts to the publishing stage. *https://bookcreator.com*
Additional Digital Story Sites	*https://storyboardthat.com* *https://pixton.com*
Empatico	Proud to be the tool to connect classrooms around the world, Empatico truly sparks kindness and empathy through literacy. Get global with your classroom! *https://empatico.org*
ThingLink	In addition to its virtual tours, ThingLink offers a way for students to annotate images and videos. *www.thinglink.com*

(continued)

FIGURE 10.6. An incomplete list of digital tools to engage readers and writers.

Resource	How it promotes joy in the literacy classroom
Nearpod	Create lessons to enhance student engagement, adding in music and videos for joy. *www.nearpod.com*
Goodreads	Who doesn't love the idea of "meeting your next favorite book?" Goodreads will use your past reading interests to keep the books coming! What a great way to #buildyourstack! *www.goodreads.com*
Weebly	Blog with your students! Not sure what to blog about? Check out these 50 new blog post ideas! *https://bit.ly/2H4viCe* *www.weebly.com*

FIGURE 10.6. *(continued)*

Stop, Think, and Take Action

Based on the ideas presented in this chapter on new literacies and technology, take time to consider the ways in which you might weave the use of technology tools into your reading and writing instruction. Reflect on the following:

If your role is that of a . . .

- **Classroom teacher** or **teacher-leader**—Think about the key pillars of literacy instruction (e.g. phonemic awareness, phonics, fluency, vocabulary, comprehension, writing, and motivation and engagement). Work with your school literacy specialist or coach to focus on one of the areas that is holding your students back. For example, perhaps a lack of phonics skills is preventing your students from being more fluent and strategic readers. Find a tool that is the right fit for your students and carve out time in your exemplary day for students to engage with this form of technology. Track successes and challenges with the support of your colleague.

- **Literacy specialist** or **literacy coach**—Seek out professional development related to new literacies and technology. If your school district has an instructional technology team, create a comprehensive and ever-changing list of digital and media technologies that can be used to help readers and writers grow.

- **School administrator** or **school-level leader**—Allocate funds for teachers to access and purchase digital read-alouds.

- **District administrator** or **district-level leader**—Survey the administrators and teachers to determine what technology tools are working and which ones need a second glance. Critically reflect on which tools are imaginatively impacting readers and writers versus valuing passive compliance. Ask yourself, "How much time are the intervention students actively reading?"

- **Professional developer**—Look at the data to determine areas of weakness by grade level. Ask yourself, "Are the digital tools being used to imaginatively and effectively address the gaps in the areas I've identified? If not, what are some potential alternatives that I can advocate for?"

Concluding Thoughts

In this book, we reiterate numerous times that we are advocates for a comprehensive approach to literacy instruction, and that helping readers and writers realize their potential is a feat that cannot be accomplished without making joy, happiness, motivation, and engagement central to the decisions we make as literacy changemakers. The paths we choose to take are laden with the reality that there will be roadblocks, but they are sprinkled with joyful reminders that we chose this profession for a reason and have a greater good on our minds. With the right people in the right seats on the bus, we can, in fact, have school communities where we can bring the joy of reading and writing back into focus for teachers and students. Let's revisit some of our literacy lessons.

First and foremost, it is important to embrace the ideals of shared leadership. A commitment to our students and their potential as readers and writers involves:

- school leaders,
- literacy specialists and coaches,
- district supervisors and administrators,
- data-driven specialists,
- teachers,
- librarians/media specialists,
- support staff,
- parents,
- board of education members,
- college/university consultants, and
- anyone else who shares a passion for developing readers and writers.

These teams need to have a common purpose or "why" for the literacy work ahead of them and commit to a joyful passion for teaching and learning, while forging consensus, building literacy knowledge and expertise, involving diverse voices from the school community, and keeping students' needs centered when decisions are made. In some instances, these recommendations might seem like a "no-brainer" for actively advocating for readers and writers, but we witness all too often how these ingredients for a literacy-strong leadership team are not in place in school communities that serve students. As shown in our design for the exemplary literacy day and in our experience with helping schools realize its potential, we suggest aiming for the ideal.

How can this work be done?

- Don't lose sight of changing classroom practices **with special attention paid to joy and engagement.** Teaching is demanding work, yet many teachers report they are mostly happy in their jobs. Let's learn from the most successful literacy environments and continue to network and collaborate on behalf of kids.
- Continue to bring in experts to model the teaching practices you wish to implement, but do so with a collaborative team effort. Through this collaboration, you will be able to assemble an internal team of literacy leaders capable of guiding and leading future professional development that is supplemented by outside experts rather than being entirely driven by them!

Changemaking, by definition, is an attempt to better the world. It involves gathering resources, producing and contributing to knowledge, and understanding the world in which we live. As a literacy changemaker, you will always be on the cutting edge of what is current and effective, but likely and proudly identify as a lifelong learner as well. As we collaborated to write this book, we reflected on the ideals of the exemplary literacy day, but continued to live and learn to realize a number of important points:

- You must, no matter what, find your literacy "square squad," "power posse," or any other term you assign to shared leadership teams. Articulate your "why," and keep the exemplary literacy day and research-based best practices in focus.
- It is important to protect every child's rights to read and rights to excellent literacy instruction. A number of unstoppable movements that mobilize the power and impact of such commitments are taking place. Stay joyful, stay engaged, and your students will follow.
- Don't hold back from taking an honest look at your literacy approaches. Dive into your data with an eye toward constant improvement. In the words of International Literacy Association (ILA) President Stephen Peters, let's choose "better" practices, if not best. Emphasizing professional development and opportunities for professional learning and buy-in from teachers will support continuous improvement for readers and writers.
- Calibrate and/or recalibrate your practices for learning environments, early literacy, adolescent learners, multilingual learners, family literacy, and new literacies. There is a profound joy in knowing that we never stop learning and growing.

This book was designed to motivate teachers to refocus joy for students and literacy learning. Of course, we strongly believe that teachers must also protect their own time to recharge and recommit to this worthwhile work. In many instances, this involves practicing exactly what we preach: setting aside time for joyful choice reading. As you protect every child's rights to read, set aside your own time to rejuvenate, or to do whatever it takes to refocus your efforts on comprehensive literacy teaching and learning. We know that one of the most important elements in literacy development is a teacher who encourages children to want to read and write. We are surrounded by skills and strategies, but need to comprehensively equip students with phonemic awareness, phonics, fluency, vocabulary, comprehension, and writing opportunities. Our students also need to be motivated, engaged, and reminded of the *joy* that comes with being lifelong readers and writers. *That joy begins with you, the changemaker. Get connected, stay connected. We can't wait to hear about the amazing difference you are making on behalf of readers and writers!*

With gratitude,
Ken, Maureen, and Rachel

References

Adoniou, M. (2019). *Teaching and assessing spelling.* Newark, DE: International Literacy Association.

Allington, R. (2002). What I've learned about effective reading instruction: From a decade of studying exemplary elementary classroom teachers. *Phi Delta Kappan, 83*(10), 740–747.

Barone, D., & Wright, T. E. (2008). Literacy instruction with digital and media technologies. *The Reading Teacher, 62*(4), 292–302.

Bear, D. R., Invernizzi, M., Templeton, S., & Johnston, F. (2008). *Words their way: Word study for phonics, vocabulary, and spelling instruction* (4th ed.). Upper Saddle River, NJ: Pearson.

Beck, I. L., McKeown, M. G., & Kucan, L. (2013). *Bringing words to life: Robust vocabulary instruction* (2nd ed.). New York: Guilford Press.

Bishop, R. S. (1990). Mirrors, windows, and sliding glass doors. *Perspectives, 6*(3), ix–xi.

Blanchard, K., & Bowles, S. (1998). *Gung ho!: Turn on the people in any organization.* New York: William Morrow.

Blauman, L., & Burke, J. (2017). *Your literacy standards companion: What they mean and how to teach them, grades 3–5.* Thousand Oaks, CA: Corwin.

Blevins, W. (2019). *Meeting the challenges of early literacy phonics instruction.* Newark, DE: International Literacy Association.

Block, C., & Mangieri, J. N. (2006). *The vocabulary-enriched classroom: Practices for improving the reading performance of all students in grades 3 and up.* New York: Scholastic.

Booksource. (2019). Inclusive classroom library checklist. Retrieved from *www.booksource.com/inclusive-classroom-library-checklist.*

Brown, B. (2018). *Dare to lead: Brave work. Tough conversations. Whole hearts.* New York: Penguin Random House.

Burke, J. (2017a). *Your literacy standards companion: What they mean and how to teach them, grades 6–8.* Thousand Oaks, CA: Corwin.

Burke, J. (2017b). *Your literacy standards companion: What they mean and how to teach them, grades 9–12.* Thousand Oaks, CA: Corwin.

Carris, J. (2011). Reconceptualization: Inclusive and empowering literacy education for non-reading adolescents. *Counterpoints, 361,* 113–133. Retrieved from *www.jstor.org/stable/42980919.*

Chiaet, J. (2013, October 4). Novel finding: Reading literary fiction improves empathy. Retrieved from *www.scientificamerican.com/article/novel-finding-reading-literary-fiction-improves-empathy.*

Clark, R. (2015). *Move your bus: An extraordinary new approach to accelerating success in work and life.* New York: Touchstone.

Cockley, K. (2016). *Joy in reading: A middle school literacy enrichment program.* Westerville, OH: Association for Middle Level Education.

Colorín Colorado. (2019). ¡Colorín Colorado!: A bilingual site for educators and families of English language learners. Retrieved from *www.colorincolorado.org.*

Cunningham, K. E. (2019). *Start with joy: Designing literacy learning for student happiness.* Portsmouth, NH: Stenhouse.

Cunningham, P. (2017). *Phonics they use: Words for reading and writing.* Boston: Pearson.

Cunningham, P., & Allington, R. (2015). *Classrooms that work: They can all read and write* (6th ed.). Boston: Pearson.

Diller, D. (2008). *Spaces and places.* Portsmouth, NH: Stenhouse.

DuFour, R., DuFour, R., Eaker, R., Many, T. W., & Mattos, M. (2016). *Learning by doing: A handbook for professional learning communities at work.* Bloomington, IN: Solution Tree.

Dwyer, B., Kern, D., & Williams, J. (2019). *Children's rights to excellent literacy instruction.* Newark, DE: International Literacy Association.

Dwyer, B., Kunz, K., & Simpson, A. (2019). *Right to integrated support systems.* Newark, DE: International Literacy Association.

Eckert, J. (2016). Bring joy back into the classroom. *Education Week, 35*(26), 21.

Edwards, P. A. (2009). *Tapping the potential of parents.* New York: Scholastic.

Ehri, L. C. (2004). Teaching phonemic awareness and phonics: An explanation of the National Reading Panel meta-analyses. In P. McCardle & V. Chhabra (Eds.), *The voice of evidence in reading research* (pp. 153–186). Baltimore, MD: Brookes.

Finchler, J., & O'Malley, K. (2010). *Miss Malarkey leaves no reader behind.* New York: Bloomsbury.

Fisher, D., & Frey, N. (2015). *Text-dependent questions, grades K–5: Pathways to close and critical reading.* Thousand Oaks, CA: Corwin.

Fisher, D., Frey, N., & Hattie, J. (2016). *Visible learning for literacy.* Thousand Oaks, CA: Corwin.

Fisher, D., Frey, N., Quaglia, R., Smith, D., & Lande, L. (2018). *Engagement by design: Creating learning environments where students thrive.* Thousand Oaks, CA: Corwin.

Fullan, M., & Quinn, J. (2016). *Coherence: The right drivers in action for schools, districts, and systems.* Thousand Oaks, CA: Corwin.

Giroir, S., Grimaldo, L. R., Vaughn, S., & Roberts, G. (2015). Interactive read-alouds for English learners in the elementary grades. *The Reading Teacher, 68*(8), 639–648.

Guthrie, J. (Ed.). (2008). *Engaging adolescents in reading.* Thousand Oaks, CA: Corwin.

International Literacy Association. (2018a). *What's hot in literacy.* Newark, DE: Author.

International Literacy Association. (2018b). Why literacy? Retrieved from *www.literacyworldwide.org/about-us/why-literacy.*

International Literacy Association. (2019a). *Advocating for children's rights to read.* Newark, DE: Author.

International Literacy Association. (2019b). *Literacy Leadership Brief: Creating Passionate Readers Through Independent Reading.* Newark, DE: Author.

Kittle, P. (2013). *Book love: Developing depth, stamina, and passion in adolescent readers.* Portsmouth, NH: Heinemann.

Koutrakos, P. (2019). *Word study that sticks.* Thousand Oaks, CA: Corwin.

Lee & Low Books. (2017). Classroom Library Questionnaire. Retrieved from *www.leeandlow.com/uploads/loaded_document/408/Classroom-Library-Questionnaire_FINAL.pdf.*

Lemons, C. J., Allor, J. H., Al Otaiba, S., & LeJeune, L. M. (2016). 10 research-based tips for enhancing literacy instruction for students with intellectual disability. *Teaching Exceptional Children, 49*(1), 18–30.

Lewis-Spector, J., & Jay, A. B. (2011). Leadership for literacy in the 21st century [White paper]. Retrieved August 1, 2019, from *www.aleronline.org/resource/resmgr/files/aler_white_paper_on_literacy.pdf.*

Linder, R. (2014). *K–2 chart sense: Common sense charts to teach K–2 informational texts and literature.* Atlanta, GA: Literacy Initiative.

Lloyd, S. C., & Harwin, A. (2019, September 3). In national ranking of school systems, a new state is on top. Retrieved from *www.edweek.org/ew/articles/2019/09/04/new-jersey-tops-national-ranking-of-schools.html?cmp=soc-edit-tw.*

McLaughlin, C. (2016). The lasting impact of mispronouncing students' names. Retrieved from *http://neatoday.org/2016/09/01/pronouncing-students-names.*

Morrow, L. M. (2020). *Literacy development in the early years: Helping children read and write* (9th ed.). Boston: Pearson.

Morrow, L. M., Kunz, K., & Hall, M. (2018). *Breaking through the language arts block: Organizing and managing the exemplary literacy day.* New York: Guilford Press.

Mulderig, E. A. (1992). *Tiny the tree frog tours Bermuda.* Hamilton, Bermuda: Bermudian Publishing.

National Center for Education Statistics. (2019). *English language learners in public schools.* Washington, DC: U.S. Department of Education.

National Endowment for the Arts. (2007). To read or not to read: A question of national consequence. Retrieved from *www.arts.gov/sites/default/files/ToRead.pdf.*

National Reading Panel Report. (2000). *Report of the National Reading Panel: Teaching children to read.* Washington, DC: National Institute of Child Health and Human Development.

Nesloney, T., & Welcome, A. (2016). *Kids deserve it!: Pushing boundaries and challenging conventional thinking.* San Diego, CA: Dave Burgess Consulting.

New Jersey Department of Education. (2019). New Jersey student learning standards. Retrieved from *www.state.nj.us/education/cccs/2016/ela.*

Nielson, L. F. (2008). *Mrs. Muddle's holidays.* New York: Farrar, Straus & Giroux.

O'Connor, R. E. (2011). Phoneme awareness and the alphabetic principle. In R. E. O'Connor & P. F. Vadasy (Eds.), *Handbook of reading interventions* (pp. 9–26). New York: Guilford Press.

O'Donnell, A. (2017, October 5). Celebrating literacy leadership: John Guthrie. Retrieved from *www.literacyworldwide.org/blog/literacy-daily/2017/10/05/celebrating-literacy-leadership-john-guthrie.*

Overturf, B., Montgomery, L. H., & Smith, M. H. (2013). *Word nerds: Teaching all students to learn and love vocabulary.* Portsmouth, NH: Stenhouse.

Overturf, B., Montgomery, L. H., & Smith, M. H. (2015). *Vocabularians: Integrated word study in the middle grades.* Portsmouth, NH: Stenhouse.

Paciga, K. A., O'Brien, L. M., Kucirkova, N., & O'Clair, A. (2019). *Digital resources in early childhood literacy development.* Newark, DE: International Literacy Association.

Pearson, P. D. (2019, October). *What research really says about teaching reading.* Paper presented at the meeting of the International Literacy Association, New Orleans, LA.

Purkey, W. W., & Novak, J. (1996). *Inviting school success: A self-concept approach to teaching, learning, and democratic practice* (3rd. ed.). New York: Wadsworth.

Quaglia Institute. (2019). Student voice: A decade of data. Retrieved from *http://quagliainstitute.org/dmsView/Student_Voice_Grades_6-12_Decade_of_Data_Report*.

Reading Rockets. (2019). Launching young readers! Retrieved from *www.readingrockets.org*.

Rhode Island Teachers of English Language Learners. (n.d.). Languages of Rhode Island: Language and country projects. Retrieved from *www.ritell.org/Language-and-Country-Projects*.

Routman, R. (2003). *Reading essentials*. Portsmouth, NH: Heinemann.

Rubin, G. (2015). *The happiness project: Or, why I spent a year trying to sing in the morning, clean my closets, fight right, read Aristotle, and generally have more fun*. New York: Harper.

Scholastic. (2019a). *Kids and family reading report* (7th ed.). New York: Author.

Scholastic. (2019b). Classroom library checklist. Retrieved from *www.scholastic.com/content/dam/teachers/migrated-assets-not-associated-with-content/migrated-pdfs-and-other-files/classroom_library_checklist.pdf*.

Sibberson, F. (2018, June 26). Build your stack: Read-aloud recommendations. Retrieved from *www2.ncte.org/blog/2018/06/build-your-stack-read-aloud-recommendations*.

Sincero, J. (2018). *You are a badass every day: How to keep your motivation strong, your vibe high, and your quest for transformation unstoppable*. New York: Penguin Random House.

Singer, T. W. (2018). *EL excellence every day: The flip-to guide for differentiating academic literacy*. Thousand Oaks, CA: Corwin.

Singer, T. W. (n.d.). Tonya Ward Singer: Courageous learning. Retrieved from *https://tonyasinger.com*.

Smith, C. B. (1991). Literature for gifted and talented. *The Reading Teacher, 44*(8), 608–609.

Stahl, K., & Bravo, M. (2010). Contemporary classroom vocabulary assessment for content areas. *The Reading Teacher, 63*(7), 566–578.

Stahl, K. A., Flanigan, K., & McKenna, M. C. (2020). *Assessment for reading instruction* (4th ed.). New York: Guilford Press.

Stanberry, K., & Swanson, L. (2009). Effective reading interventions for kids with learning disabilities. Retrieved *from www.readingrockets.org/article/effective-reading-interventions-kids-learning-disabilities*.

Taberski, S., & Burke, J. (2017). *Your literacy standards companion: What they mean and how to teach them, grades K–2*. Thousand Oaks, CA: Corwin.

TED Talk. (2009, October 7). The danger of a single story. Retrieved from *www.youtube.com/watch?v=D9Ihs241zeg&t=42s*.

Terada, Y. (2019, February 27). The key to effective classroom management. Retrieved from *www.edutopia.org/article/key-effective-classroom-management*.

University of Oxford. (2011, May 9). Reading at 16 linked to better job prospects. Retrieved from *www.sciencedaily.com/releases/2011/05/110504150539.htm*.

U.S. Department of Education, Office for Civil Rights, & U.S. Department of Justice, Civil Rights Division. (2015). Dear colleague letter: English learner students and limited English proficient parents. Retrieved from *www2.ed.gov/about/offices/list/ocr/letters/colleague-el-201501.pdf*.

U.S. Department of Education. Office of Educational Research and Improvement, National Center for Education Statistics. (2002). The Nation's Report Card: U.S.

History 2001, NCES 2002-483, by M. S. Lapp, W. S. Grigg, & B. S.-H. Tay-Lim. Washington, DC.

Valdés, G. (n.d.). Multilingualism. Retrieved from *www.linguisticsociety.org/resource/multi-lingualism*.

Visible Learning. (2018). Collective teacher efficacy (CTE) according to John Hattie. Retrieved from *https://visible-learning.org/2018/03/collective-teacher-efficacy-hattie*.

Willis, J. (2007). The neuroscience of joyful education. Retrieved from *www.ascd.org/publications/educational-leadership/summer07/vol64/num09/The-Neuroscience-of-Joyful-Education.aspx*.

Yamada, K. (2018). What do you do with a chance? Retrieved from *www.youtube.com/watch?v=0_fYv3UrSlQ*.

Index